With the Judeans in the Palestine Campaign

J. H. Patterson

With the Judeans in the Palestine Campaign

ISBN: 978-1-64799-577-5

PREFACE

The formation of a Battalion of Jews for service in the British Army is an event without precedent in our annals, and the part played by such a unique unit is assured of a niche in history owing to the fact that it fought in Palestine, not only for the British cause, but also for the Restoration of the Jewish people to the Promised Land.

In writing the following narrative, my object has been to give a faithful account of the doings of this Jewish Battalion while it was under my command.

I am much indebted to Captain H. Davis, the Rev. L. A. Falk, Mr. Bendov of Jerusalem, and Canon Parfit for permission to reproduce the photographs illustrating this book, which add considerably to its interest.

J. H. P.
London, 1922

CONTENTS

INTRODUCTION

In the darkest days of the War, the British Cabinet decided that it would be good policy to create a Jewish Regiment, and accordingly, in August, 1917, the first Jewish Battalion was formed.

From that day forth, as a matter of duty and loyalty to King and Country, it was clearly incumbent on all those in authority to treat this new unit with justice, and do everything in their power to make it a success.

It is to be deplored that this Jewish Battalion—this ewe lamb of Israel—did not receive, while on Active Service in the Holy Land, that measure of justice and fair play that was its due.

In common with the vast majority of my countrymen I have the "fair play" sense strongly developed. I am always prone to be on the side of the under dog—more especially when I see that the poor devil is getting more kicks than in all fairness are his due. In Palestine, unfortunately, I was constantly called upon to ward off unfair blows aimed at the Jewish Battalion under my command by certain members of the local staff of the Egyptian Expeditionary Force.

I have passed over many of our sufferings in silence, and no record of them will be found in this book, but I am afraid they have left an indelible mark in the mind and heart of every man who served in the Jewish Battalion under my command, and I fear that the evil effects of the local Military Administration will reverberate throughout Palestine for many a long year.

But before I proceed further, let me first of all make it clearly understood that I am not a Jew,—indeed, at the outbreak of the Great War I knew nothing of this ancient people, always excepting what I had read about them in the Bible, and other Jewish books. My first contact with Jews was in the Gallipoli campaign, where I was sent in command of a Corps composed of Zionists who had escaped from Palestine at the outbreak of war and taken service with the British Forces. Presumably because I had had this experience, I was appointed to the command of the first Jewish Infantry unit raised for service with the British Army. The career of such a unique unit is bound to be closely followed by all Jews, while it would not surprise me if the historian of the future seizes upon this dramatic appearance of the Jewish warrior, fighting for the redemption of Israel under the banner of England, as one of the most interesting episodes of the great World War.

Unfortunately for us, with a few honourable exceptions, the local Staff of the E.E.F. were "troublers of Israel." Instead of furthering the policy of the Home Government by holding out a helping hand to this new unit, on the contrary every obstacle was placed in its way.

In our times of tribulation in the Holy Land, my thoughts often went back to the Dardanelles, and I was heartened and cheered by the remembrance of the vastly different treatment meted out to the Jewish soldiers by the Staff in Gallipoli. Sir Ian Hamilton had vision enough to foresee what a tremendous force would be won over to the cause of England by dealing justly with Israel. In the Mediterranean Expeditionary Force the attitude was essentially British. I regret I cannot say the same of the Staff of the Egyptian Expeditionary Force in 1918 and 1919.

I am happy to be able to put on record that the Battalion was treated fairly and justly all the time it was stationed in England. The Staff at Plymouth always held out a helping hand when needed, and we embarked for Egypt with the blessing of the War Office, and of the Adjutant-General, Sir Nevil Macready, who told us before we sailed that it was his aim to form a Jewish Brigade, and that he was writing to the Commander-in-Chief of the E.E.F. to recommend that this should be done as soon as our numbers justified such a step.

I felt that the Adjutant-General had confided a great trust to me when I was selected for the command of this Jewish unit. It was a complete change from the command of an Irish Battalion, but the Irishman and the Jew have much in common—temperament, generosity, love of children, devotion to parents, readiness to help those down on their luck, and, be it noted, great personal bravery. These qualities will probably not appear out of place to my readers so far as the Irishman is concerned, but I imagine many will be surprised when they hear that they also apply to the Jew. It is true, however, and so should be more widely known. The soul-stirring deeds on the battlefield of such heroes as Judas Maccabæus, Bar Kochba, and many others can never be forgotten.

I had one fear when I took over command of the Judæans, and that was that I might not be able to do them justice. I felt that, if a suitable Jewish officer could be found, it would be more appropriate that he should have the honour of leading these soldiers of Israel in the struggle for the redemption of Palestine; but, although I publicly stated that I should be glad to see a Jewish officer appointed to the command, no one came forward, and I was left with the whole weight of this great responsibility to the Jewish people on my shoulders. I therefore made up my mind, from the moment I took command, that, so far as was humanly possible, the

Jewish Battalion should be brought through its fiery ordeal with honour.

It was unfortunate for the new Regiment, and doubly unfortunate for the Jewish people in Palestine, as this narrative will show, that the attitude of the local Staff was diametrically opposed to the declared policy of His Majesty's Government, which had announced to the world, in the famous Balfour Declaration, that Palestine should once again become a National Home for the Jewish people. In the face of this British announcement, certain officials in the Holy Land acted as if this epoch-making Declaration were nothing but a mere "scrap of paper."

When I observed the vain strivings of these men, and remembered the Promise to Israel, I called to mind the saying of Gamaliel, the great Rabbi, "If this work be of men it will come to naught, but if it be of God, ye cannot overthrow it."

This local anti-Jewish policy eventually culminated in the Jerusalem pogrom, described at the close of this book, when, under British rule, murderous native mobs ran riot, practically unchecked, for nearly three days within the walls of the City.

This deplorable outrage at last opened the eyes of the Imperial Authorities to what was going on in Palestine, with the result that the Military Administration was abolished. A competent civil Governor replaced the Military Administrator, and Sir Herbert Samuel was sent out to pour oil and wine into the wounds which the unfortunate Jewish inhabitants had received, and to carry out the declared policy of England as announced in the Balfour Declaration.

CHAPTER I

THE BALFOUR DECLARATION

In the early days of 1917 the outlook for the Allied Powers was particularly black and menacing. England, the mainstay in the great struggle, was in deadly peril, for, just about this time, the ruthless Submarine campaign was at its height and our shipping losses were appalling.

The Central Powers, with startling rapidity, had crushed and overrun Belgium, Serbia, and Roumania, and a large slice of France was in the grip of the invader. It was a case of stalemate with Italy, while Russia, the Colossus with the feet of clay, was in the throes of a Revolution and lost to the Allies.

Turkey, the so-called "sick man of Europe," was found not only able to "sit up and take nourishment," but strong enough to administer some nasty knocks to the surgeon, as we discovered to our cost in Gallipoli, and other places in the Near East.

The Great Republic of the West did indeed throw in her lot with us in April, 1917, but many perilous months would have to elapse before she could pull her full weight, or even make her enormous power felt to any appreciable extent on the battlefields of Europe.

At such a moment as this it was of the very greatest importance that the world should be carefully scanned, and every available ideal and policy made use of, which could be of advantage to our righteous cause.

The happy inspiration thereupon seized upon our Ministers to win over to the side of the Allies the teeming millions of the Children of Israel scattered throughout the world.

The restoration of these people to the land of their forefathers had long been engaging the thoughts of mankind, and our Statesmen now felt that the time was ripe for this age-long issue to be brought to fruition.

It was of course known to the leading Zionists that the British Government was considering the policy of making a pronouncement in favour of the Jewish people, and many of the leaders of Zionism, such as Dr. Weizmann, Mr. Sokolow, Mr. Jabotinsky, Mr. Joseph Cowen, etc., lost no opportunity of pressing home the importance of winning Jewry, the world over, to England's side, by declaring boldly for a Jewish Palestine.

1

It was felt by many that the right and proper way for Jewry to help England was by raising a Jewish Legion to aid in the redemption of Palestine, and of this movement the leading spirit was Vladimir Jabotinsky, a distinguished orator, author, and journalist.

Ever since the beginning of the War this remarkable man, a Jew from Russia, had carried on a vigorous propaganda on behalf of England. At his own expense, he had founded a newspaper in Copenhagen, and distributed it broadcast among Jews in Russia, Poland, neutral countries, America, etc.

His propaganda was of great value to the Allies, for the Jews naturally hated Russia, owing to their harsh treatment and persecution in that country, and it was not until Jabotinsky set to work that they perceived that their real interests lay with the Allies.

To show a good example to others, he enlisted as a private in the 20th Battalion London Regiment, where he gathered round him a platoon composed principally of men who had recently been serving in Gallipoli in the Zion Mule Corps.

From his humble position in the ranks he bombarded the Prime Minister, and the Secretaries of State for War and Foreign Affairs in this country; he sent emissaries to America, North and South, to Russia, Poland, the Caucasus, etc., and when, in July, 1917, the Government declared their intention of creating a Jewish Regiment, he had everything in train for the formation of a legion at least 50,000 strong.

I mention this here as one instance of this gallant officer's efforts for England, and I will ask the reader to make a mental note of it, for before this narrative is ended it will be my painful duty to show how Jabotinsky was rewarded for all his invaluable services to the British cause.

The Government policy towards world Jewry was brought to a head by a vigorous Zionist offensive, and resulted in the creation of a Jewish Battalion in August, 1917, followed a little later by the famous Balfour Declaration in favour of a National Home for the Jewish people in Palestine.

This bold and wise pronouncement of British policy was of great and far-reaching importance, and is regarded by Jewry throughout the world as their Charter of Liberty.

It is embodied in the following letter to Lord Rothschild:—

Foreign Office,
2nd November, 1917.

2

Dear Lord Rothschild,

I have much pleasure in conveying to you on behalf of H.M.'s Government, the following Declaration of sympathy with Jewish Zionist aspirations, which has been submitted to and approved by the Cabinet:

His Majesty's Government view with favour the establishment in Palestine of a National Home for the Jewish people, and will use their best endeavours to facilitate the achievement of this object, *it being clearly understood that nothing shall be done which may prejudice the civil and religious rights of existing non-Jewish communities in Palestine, or the rights and political status enjoyed by Jews in any other country.*

I should be grateful if you would bring this Declaration to the knowledge of the Zionist Federation.

Yours sincerely,
(Signed) Arthur James Balfour.

This was, perhaps, the most momentous Declaration made throughout the War, and it derived a special significance from the fact that it was made just at the time when the first definite steps were being taken towards freeing Palestine from the yoke of the Turk. It was received by practically all sections of the British Press with the most cordial approval.

By pious Jews it was regarded as little short of the Voice of God, bringing their long-cherished aspirations within sight of fulfilment.

All down the centuries from the time of the Dispersion it has been the dream of the Jew that one day he would be restored to his ancestral home. In his exile the age-long cry of his stricken soul has ever been "next year in Jerusalem."

Christians too have always believed in the fulfilment of prophecy, and the Restoration of the Jewish people is of no little interest to them, so it can be imagined with what feelings of joy and gratitude the masses of the Jewish people looked upon this promise of England, holding out as it did the prospect of the realization of their dearest hope. Nothing like it has been known since the days of King Cyrus. It is not too much to say that this epoch-making Declaration uplifted the soul of Israel the world over.

Sir Arthur Balfour may not live to see the full fruits of his famous pronouncement, but prophecy will assuredly be fulfilled, and his name will go down for all time, second only to that of Cyrus, in the Chronicles of Israel.

3

Jeremiah's prophecy on the Restoration of Israel has a wonderful significance in these days: "Hear the word of the Lord, O ye nations, and declare it in the isles afar off, and say, He that scattered Israel will gather him and keep him, as a Shepherd doth his flock."

CHAPTER II

THE SANBALLATS

On the 27th July, 1917, while I was stationed at the Curragh in command of a Battalion of the Royal Dublin Fusiliers, I got a telegram from the War Office ordering me to report there and commence the organization of the Jewish Legion about to be raised, so I set out forthwith for London.

On getting my instructions from Major-General R. Hutchison, the Director of Organization, he told me, among other things, that a certain Sergeant Jabotinsky would probably be most useful to me, for he was a very keen worker and an ardent advocate of the Jewish Regiment. I told him that I had already met Jabotinsky, and I knew his assistance would be invaluable, and requested that he might be attached to me for duty at once.

I was given a room at the War Office Annexe which had been taken over from the National Liberal Club. Here I was joined in due course by Jabotinsky, now a full-fledged sergeant.

We had hardly begun to move in the matter of recruiting for the Jewish Regiment, when I became aware that in certain quarters of influential English Jewry there was violent hostility to Zionist aspirations, and also to the very idea of a Jewish Regiment.

I therefore felt that, in order to clear the air, it would be necessary to hold a meeting of those who were in favour of, as well as those who were opposed to, the formation of a Jewish Regiment, and try to induce the latter to cease obstructing a policy which had already been decided upon by the British Government, and to give me their help in making the proposed Regiment a success.

A meeting of representative men on both sides was held at the War Office on the 8th August, 1917. Among those present were:

Lord Rothschild, Major Lionel de Rothschild, Major Neil Primrose, Captain Ormsby Gore, M.P., Mr. Sebag Montefiore, Dr. Weizmann, Mr. Joseph Cowen, Dr. Eder, Captain Salaman, R.A.M.C., Mr. M. J. Landa, Mr. L. J. Greenberg, the Rev. S. Lipson (Senior Jewish Chaplain to the Forces in England), and Sergeant Jabotinsky—about twenty in all. Colonel Sir Mark Sykes, M.P. (whose untimely death I deeply lament), and Lieut.-Colonel L. S. Amery, M.P., who were then Secretaries to the War Cabinet, also attended, both being warm friends of the movement.

I briefly addressed the meeting and explained that I had called them together to give me their advice and assistance in the formation of the Jewish Regiment.

I was, of course, aware that there was somewhat of a cleavage amongst the Jews on this question, but the bitterness and hostility shown was quite a revelation to me. I could not understand how any Jew could fail to grasp this Heaven-sent opportunity and do all in his power to further the efforts of the British Government on behalf of the Jewish people.

Imagine my surprise, therefore, when certain of the Jews in opposition vigorously denounced the formation of a Jewish Regiment, and equally vigorously damned the aspirations of the Zionists!

Dr. Weizmann gave a slashing reply to the Sanballats from the Zionist point of view which cut the ground from under their feet; and Jabotinsky, in his address for the cause he had at heart, lifted the debate to a level immeasurably above the point of view of his opponents.

A few others spoke, and then I again addressed the meeting and said I thought it was a good thing the Government had not left it to the community to form a Jewish Regiment, for I saw that they would never agree; but, as the Government had already made up its mind, and was determined to have a Jewish Legion of some kind, I begged them to lay aside all differences and help me to make a success of a movement which was bound to affect Jews, one way or another, throughout the world. In conclusion, I said I would rather know who were my friends, and asked all those who did not intend to further this scheme, which after all was a scheme propounded and adopted by the British Government, to retire. Not a man moved.

While I was making my address a note was passed to me from hand to hand. On opening it I read, "Can you dine with me this evening? I should like to join your new Battalion. N.P." I little knew when I scribbled back: "So sorry, am engaged," what serious consequences hung on my answer, for I feel sure that Neil Primrose

5

would not have been cut off in his prime had I dined with him that night and "recruited" him for the Jewish Battalion, but I never saw this very gallant officer again. He went out to Palestine soon afterwards, where he met his death while leading his men in a charge.

To return to the meeting: when I found that not one of our opponents was prepared to declare himself an open enemy of the policy of H.M.'s Government, I said that as the formation of the various Committees connected with the Regiment was an essentially Jewish matter I would now retire, and I asked Lord Rothschild to take the Chair.

Within half an hour I was summoned by Brigadier-General Sir Auckland Geddes, as he then was. The General appeared to be extremely flurried and annoyed. Apparently, immediately after I had left the meeting, two gentlemen had gone straight from it to Sir Auckland, and made a bitter attack on me for having, as they said, held a Zionist Meeting in the War Office.

I assured him that there was no attempt at holding a Zionist meeting, but that a number of representative Jews and others had been called to help me in carrying out the policy of the War Office, and I pointed out that it was entirely due to the two gentlemen who complained, that any question of Zionism had been raised.

Why any Jew should be an anti-Zionist passes my comprehension, for the Zionist ideal in no way interferes with the rights and privileges of those fortunate Jews who have found happy homes in friendly countries, but aims at establishing a national home for those less happy ones, who, against their will, are forced to live in exile, and who have never ceased to yearn for the land promised to their forefather Abraham and his seed for ever.

Yet I will have to show that, as there were Sanballats[1] who bitterly opposed the restoration in the days of King Artaxerxes 2,500 years ago, so there were modern Sanballats who bitterly opposed the restoration in the days of King George.

---

[1] See Nehemiah, Chapters 3 and 4.

6

CHAPTER III

THE FORMATION OF THE JEWISH REGIMENT

On the 23rd August, 1917, the formation of the "Jewish Regiment" was officially announced in the London Gazette, and I was appointed to the command of a Battalion.

At the same time it was officially intimated that a special Jewish name and badge would be given to the Battalions of this Regiment.

On hearing of this determination the Sanballats immediately got very busy. Heads were put together, and letters written up and down the land to all and sundry who were likely to serve their purpose, with the result that, on the 30th August, 1917, a deputation waited upon Lord Derby (then Secretary of State for War), for the purpose of making representations against the proposed name and badge of the Jewish Regiment, and, in fact, against the formation of any such unit as a Jewish Battalion.

One member of this Deputation went so far as to represent to Lord Derby that Lord Rothschild, the head of the celebrated Jewish family, to whom, as representing the Jewish people, Mr. Balfour later on addressed the famous declaration, was also opposed to the formation of a Jewish Regiment.

Lord Rothschild assured me that this was not the case; for, once it became the policy of the British Government to form a Jewish Regiment, he felt bound as a patriotic Jew to back it up and do all in his power to make it a success. No little thanks are due to Lord Rothschild for the way he devoted himself to the comfort and welfare of the Jewish Battalions, from the first day they were formed.

The result of the Deputation was that the name "Jewish Regiment" was abolished, and no Jewish badge was sanctioned. All Jewish Battalions raised were to be called "Royal Fusiliers."

But our worthy friends might have saved themselves all the trouble they took, and the trouble they gave to the War Ministry, because, from the moment that the battalions were formed, although they were known officially as Royal Fusiliers, yet unofficially, everywhere, and by every person, they were known solely as the Jewish Battalions.

Lord Derby made the mistake of thinking that these few rich men represented the Jewish masses. A greater mistake was never made, for, from my own experience, I can vouch for the fact that they are altogether out of touch with the thoughts and feelings of the vast majority of the Jewish people.

What a different tale I should have to tell had men such as these played up to the policy of England. Had their vision only been broader, they would have said among themselves, "This is a policy we do not like. It may affect us adversely, but it is the policy of England, and England in peril, and we must therefore bind ourselves together and make it a success."

If they feared that these Jews from Russia and Poland would not worthily uphold Jewish traditions, they might have gone to the Secretary for War and told him their fears, and said that, as it was absolutely necessary for world Jewry that this experiment of creating Jewish Battalions should have a fair chance, they would request his aid in this matter, and ask that at least twenty-five per cent. of every battalion be composed of Jews from England, who, having seen service in France, would therefore give some necessary and valuable stiffening to these raw Jewish units.

With such a stiffening, and a solid English Jewry at the back of the Jewish Regiment, what a triumphant page in Jewish history these battalions would have written!

Instead of this, every possible obstacle was placed in the way of success. Interested parties scoured the East end of London and the big provincial cities, advising young Jews not to enlist. Even in France the Jewish soldiers serving in the various units there were told by Jews who ought to have known better that they should on no account transfer. The result of this was that recruiting went on very slowly, and instead of being able to form a Jewish legion in the course of a few weeks, as could easily have been done out of the 40,000 Jewish young men in England alone, it took over four months to form even one battalion.

I happened by chance one day to meet a prominent member of the Sanballat deputation in the War Office, and, in the course of conversation, I asked him why he objected so strongly to the formation of a Jewish Regiment. He replied that he had no faith in the Russian Jews, and feared they would bring discredit on Jewry. I said that, from what I had seen in Gallipoli of the Jew from Russia, I had more faith in him than he had, and that I felt confident I could make him into a good soldier. He was kind enough to remark, "Well, perhaps under you they will turn out to be good soldiers, but then they might win Palestine, and I don't want to be sent there to live." I replied that his fears in this respect were entirely groundless. He remarked that he was not so sure about that, for if the Jews had a country of their own, pressure might be brought to bear upon

8

them to go and live there—which clearly shows that these rich and fortunate Jews cannot have given much real thought to the question, for there is nothing in the Zionist movement to force anyone to live in Palestine, and it would be manifestly impossible to pack 14,000,000 of people within the narrow limits of their ancestral home.

When my pessimistic friend told me that these foreign Jews were no good, and would bring discredit upon the best part of Jewry, I made a mental resolve that I would prove to him one day that his despised Jewish brethren, from Russia and elsewhere, would make as good soldiers, and as good all-round men, as those in any unit of the British Army. As these pages progress, and the history of the 38th Jewish Battalion is unfolded before the eyes of the reader, it will be seen that my expectations were more than realised, for the Battalion drilled, marched, fought, and generally played the game as well as any battalion in the Army.

It is a curious fact that, so far as I could gather, the Inner Actions Committee of the Zionist organization, with the honoured exception of Dr. Weizmann, looked on us with suspicion. The formation of Jewish Battalions did not appeal to them. How it was possible that the leaders of Zionism should not have grasped, and taken to their hearts, this gift of Jewish Battalions from the British Government, for the furtherance of their own ends, is one of the greatest examples of ineptitude that have ever come within my experience. Here was a body of keen and enthusiastic men, devoting their lives to the restoration of the Holy Land to its rightful owners, and yet they shied when the one essential weapon that could have given it to them was being virtually thrust into their hands.

How different would have been the position of the Zionists at the Peace Conference after the Armistice was signed if they had been able to point proudly to 50,000 Jewish troops in Palestine, instead of to the 5,000 who were actually serving there at the close of the War.

I know that Dr. Weizmann had vision enough to foresee the strength which such a legion would give to his diplomacy, but unfortunately his colleagues on the Zionist Council did not see eye to eye with him in this matter until it was too late.

I tried to do what in me lay with certain of the leaders of Zionism, and spent some time endeavouring to enthuse a devoted and spiritual Jew who was deeply interested in the Restoration; indeed, I thought I had won him over to the cause of the legion, for at times during our conversation his face lit up at the possibilities unfolded to him, but, alas, after I left him, I fear he fell away from grace!

9

Some of the Zionists, men such as Mr. Joseph Cowen, fully realised all the advantages which would accrue from a Jewish legion helping to win Palestine from the enemy, and these were eager workers towards this end.

Vladimir Jabotinsky always believed in the proverb that the Lord helps those who help themselves, and, therefore, he felt that it was essential that a Jewish legion should fight for the redemption of Israel's ancient heritage. And it was well for Jewry that Jabotinsky was a chosen instrument, because, if no Jewish troops had fought in Palestine, and no Jewish graves could be seen in the Cemetery on the Mount of Olives, and in every Military Cemetery in Egypt and Palestine, it would have been, for all time, a reproach unto Israel, and I have grave doubts whether the Peace Conference would have considered the time ripe for the Jewish people to be restored to their ancient land. I am certain of this, that if Jabotinsky's ideals of a powerful legion had been more fully realised, Dr. Weizmann's position at the table of the Peace Conference would have been immeasurably strengthened.

It must, however, be recorded for the honour of British Jewry, that the vast majority of English Jews were heartily in accord with the Government policy, and proud of the fact that, practically for the first time in Jewish history since the days of Judas Maccabæus and Bar Kochba, battalions of Jewish infantry were to be raised and led against the common enemy in Palestine.

It was also to the credit of English Jewry that a deputation representing the Jewish masses in England, sought and obtained an interview with the Secretary of State for War, with the view to the retention of a distinctive Jewish name and badge for the Battalions. This deputation was introduced on Sept. 5th by Mr. J. D. Kiley, M.P., a non-Jew, and among others the following men were present:—Captain Redcliffe Salaman, Dr. Eder, Messrs. Elkin Adler, Joseph Cowen, L. J. Greenberg, M. J. Landa, etc. Lord Derby had, however, committed himself to the first deputation, and all he could promise to the deputation representing the Jewish masses was that, if the Regiment distinguished itself in the Field, it would then be given a Jewish title and a Jewish badge. This deputation also obtained the War Secretary's sanction to the supply of Kosher food, and to the observance of Saturday as the day of rest; Lord Derby also promised that, as far as possible, all Jewish festivals should be respected, and that Jewish units would, service conditions permitting, be employed only in Palestine.

How the Battalions distinguished themselves, and won a special Jewish name and badge, will be recorded faithfully in the following pages.

CHAPTER IV

TRAINING AT PLYMOUTH

I was delighted when, at last, I got away from organization duty at the War Office, with all its worries and vicissitudes, and commenced the real active work of training a fighting Battalion of Jews.

Plymouth was the spot chosen as our training centre, and at the Crown Hill Barracks, near this famous and beautiful harbour, we commenced our military career.

A recruiting Depôt was at the same time established in London at 22, Chenies Street, where a Staff was installed under the command of Major Knowles, an excellent officer, who had previously served under me in the South African War, and who was an ardent supporter of Zionist ideals.

Recruits were received here, and fitted out with uniforms before being sent on to Plymouth. The comfort of the men while at the Depôt was ably attended to by various Committees of ladies and gentlemen, whose names will be found in the Appendix. They were fortunately in a position to give much needed financial aid to various dependents from the moment the Committees began work, for public-spirited and liberal Jews were found who gave to the good cause with both hands. Among these was Mr. Leopold Frank, who gave the princely donation of £1,000. Mr. Lionel D. Walford especially was untiring in his efforts for the welfare and happiness of every recruit who came to the Depôt, and so won the hearts of all by the personal service that he gave, day in and day out, that he was universally and affectionately known to the Judæans as "Daddy."

As a nucleus for the Jewish Battalion I arranged for the transfer of a platoon of my old Zion Mule Corps men from the 20th Battalion of the London Regiment, where they were then serving under the command of Colonel A. Pownall. My best thanks are due to this officer for the help he gave me in effecting the transfer of my old veterans. These warlike sons of Israel, not content with the laurels they had already won in Gallipoli, sought for fresh adventure in other fields, and so volunteered for service in France. On the way their ship was torpedoed and sunk by an Austrian submarine, but fortunately not a Zion man was drowned; all managed to cling on to spars and other wreckage and floated safely to a Grecian isle from

11

which they were rescued. They eventually reached England in safety, but all their personal belongings were lost.

Men soon began to arrive at Plymouth in batches of twenties and thirties, from all over the Kingdom. Many trades and professions were represented, but the vast majority were either tailors or in some way connected with the tailoring trade. I made it a practice to see every recruit as soon as he joined and find out something about his family and affairs. I also gave every man some advice as to how he was to conduct himself as a good soldier and a good Jew. The famous sculptor, Jacob Epstein, was one of my most promising recruits, and after he had served for some months in the ranks I recommended him for a commission. When the 38th Battalion left Plymouth for Palestine, Epstein remained behind with the second Jewish Battalion then formed, but owing to some bungling the commission was never granted.

The difficulties of my command were not few.

On broad religious grounds Judaism is not compatible with a soldier's life—and I may say I had many strict Jews in the Battalion; then the men were aliens, utterly unaccustomed to Army life, and with an inherent hatred of it, owing to the harsh military treatment to which the Jew in Russia was subjected; some of them did not speak English, and practically all of them hated serving any cause which might in the end help Russia; they knew also that there was a strong body of Jewish opinion in England which was hostile to the idea of a Jewish unit.

To make matters worse, the recruits came from sedentary occupations. They had never been accustomed to an out-door, open-air life, and naturally dreaded, and really felt, the strain of the hard military training which they had to undergo in those cold winter days in Plymouth.

It can be imagined, therefore, that I had no easy task before me in moulding these sons of Israel, and inspiring them with that martial ardour and esprit de corps which is so necessary, if men are to be of any use on the field of battle. I impressed upon them that strict discipline, and hard training, was not merely for my amusement or benefit, but was entirely in their own interests, so that when the day of battle came they would be fitter men and better fighters than their enemies, and with these two points in their favour the chances were that instead of getting killed, they would kill their opponents and emerge from the battle triumphant.

The men soon grasped the idea, and took to soldiering and all that it means with a hearty goodwill. I am happy to say that all difficulties were surmounted, and, at the close of the campaign, the

Battalion presented as fine and steady an appearance on Parade as any Battalion in the E.E.F.

Luckily for me, I had an able and enthusiastic staff to assist me in my endeavours. I cannot sufficiently praise the great service rendered to the Battalion, during its infant stages, by Captain Redcliffe Salaman, R.A.M.C., who was our medical officer. His knowledge of the men and of Jewish matters generally was invaluable to me.

My Adjutant, Captain Neill, had already had two years' experience in a similar position with a battalion of the Rifle Brigade. I found him to be able and diplomatic—the latter an essential quality in the handling of Jewish soldiers.

In my Second in Command, Major MacDermot, I had an officer of wide experience and high principles, who had served under my command in the Dublin Fusiliers.

In my Assistant Adjutant, Lt. B. Wolffe (whose tragic death in Palestine I shall relate in its proper place), I had an exceptionally gifted Jewish officer, hardworking, painstaking, conscientious, and all out in every way to make the Jewish Battalion a success.

I tried to induce Senior Jewish officers to join the Battalion, but I found it very hard to get volunteers, for the Senior men preferred to remain in their own British Regiments.

I was able to obtain the services of a fair number of Junior Jewish officers, and the Battalion gradually filled up in officers, N.C.O.'s and men.

I would like to mention here that, although the great majority of all ranks were Jews, yet there were some Christian officers, N.C.O.'s and one or two men. In spite of this there was never the very slightest question between us of either race or religion. All eventually became animated with one spirit—the success, welfare and good name of this Jewish Battalion.

I am glad to say that we had practically no crime to stain our record. There was not a single case of a civil offence being recorded against us all the time we were at Plymouth, which is something new in Army annals.

And yet another record was created by this unique Battalion. The Wet Canteen, where beer only was sold, had to be closed, for not a single pint was drunk all the time it was open.

The men showed wonderful quickness and aptitude in mastering the details of their military training. It came as a surprise to me to find that a little tailor, snatched from the purlieus of Petticoat Lane, who had never in all his life wielded anything more dangerous than a needle, soon became quite an adept in the use of the rifle and bayonet, and could transfix a dummy figure of the

13

Kaiser in the most approved scientific style, while negotiating a series of obstacle-trenches at the double.

I noticed that the men were particularly smart in all that they did whenever a General came along. I remember on one occasion, when we were about to be inspected, I told the men to be sure and stand steady on parade during the General Salute; I impressed upon them that it was a tradition in the British Army that, unless a Battalion stood perfectly steady at this critical moment, it would be thought lacking in discipline and smartness, and would get a bad report from the General. So zealous were my men to uphold this time-honoured tradition, that I verily believe that these wonderful enthusiasts for rigid British discipline never blinked an eyelid while the General was taking the salute. Certainly every Commander who inspected us always expressed his astonishment at the rock-like steadiness of the Jewish Battalion on parade.

During our training period at Plymouth we received many kindnesses from the Jewish community there, more especially from its President, Mr. Meyer Fredman.

In the long winter evenings we had lecturers who addressed the men on various interesting subjects. The famous and learned Rabbi Kuk of Jerusalem paid us a visit, and gave the men a stirring address on their duties as Jewish soldiers. Jabotinsky gave various lectures, one especially on Bialik, the great Jewish poet, being particularly memorable.

We had many talented music-hall and theatrical men in our ranks; our concerts were, therefore, excellent, and our concert party was in great request throughout the Plymouth district.

If there was one officer more than another who helped to promote the men's comfort, it was Lieut. E. Vandyk. He was in charge of the messing arrangements, and the Battalion was exceptionally fortunate in having a man of his experience to undertake this most exacting of all tasks.

Later on Vandyk proved himself equally capable as a leader in the field, where he was promoted to the rank of Captain.

I must not forget the kindness shown to us at Plymouth by Lady Astor, M.P., who gave us a Recreation Hut, and by Sir Arthur Yapp, the Secretary of the Y.M.C.A., who furthered our comfort in every possible way.

While we were yet at Plymouth I received orders from the War Office to form two more Jewish Battalions in addition to the 38th.

As soon as sufficient recruits justified it I recommended the Authorities to proceed with the formation of the 39th Battalion and to appoint Major Knowles, from the Depôt, to the Command. This was done, and from what I saw during the time I was in Plymouth, I

14

felt quite confident that Colonel Knowles would make an excellent commander.

Colonel Knowles was succeeded at the Depôt in London by Major Schonfield, who worked untiringly to promote the interests of the recruits, and to imbue them with a good, soldierly spirit while they were passing through his hands in Chenies Street. About the same time as Colonel Knowles was appointed, Captain Salaman so highly recommended his brother-in-law, Colonel F. D. Samuel, D.S.O., to me that I asked the Adjutant-General if this officer might be recalled from France to take charge of the training at Plymouth, and Jewish affairs there generally, after my departure for Palestine. The Adjutant-General very kindly agreed to my request, and transferred Colonel Samuel from France to Plymouth at very short notice.

Soon after I left for Palestine recommendations were made to the War Office that it would be preferable to have a Jewish officer in command of the 39th Battalion, and the result was that Colonel Samuel was appointed to the 39th Battalion in the place of Colonel Knowles. This treatment was most unfair to the latter, who had worked extremely hard and enthusiastically, both at the Depôt and during the time he held command of the 39th Battalion, where he did all the spade work and made things very easy for his successor. Colonel Knowles afterwards went to France and later on served with the North Russian Expeditionary Force.

Of course, it was all to the good to have a Jewish Commanding Officer, but it should have been arranged without doing an injustice to Colonel Knowles.

About this time Major Margolin, D.S.O., a Jewish officer attached to the Australian Forces, was transferred to the Depôt at Plymouth, and eventually replaced Colonel Samuel in the command of the 39th Battalion.

Outsiders will never be able to imagine the immense amount of trouble and detail involved in the formation of this unique unit. I must say that the War Office, and the local command at Plymouth, gave me every possible assistance. Colonel King, of the Military Secretary's Staff at the W.O., helped me through many a difficulty in getting Jewish officers brought back from France.

Colonel Graham, also of the War Office, came to my assistance whenever he could possibly do so, while the late Military Secretary, General Sir Francis Davies, under whom I had served in Gallipoli, was kindness itself.

General Hutchison, the Director of Organization, was always a tower of strength, and the Jewish Battalions owe him a heavy debt. Lieut.-Colonel Amery, M.P., and the late Sir Mark Sykes, M.P., also did what was in their power to make our thorny path smooth.

CHAPTER V

THE KOSHER PROBLEM

The only serious trouble we had in Plymouth occurred over Kosher food. As most people probably know, Jewish food has to be killed and cooked in a certain way as laid down in Jewish Law, and it is then known as "kosher," i.e. proper.

This was, of course, quite new to the Military authorities, and the Army being a very conservative machine, and, at times, a very stubborn one, they failed to see the necessity of providing special food for the Jewish troops—a curious state of mentality considering the care taken with the food of our Moslem soldiers.

I have a fairly shrewd idea that all the blame for the trouble we were put to in this matter must not rest altogether on the shoulders of the Army officials, for I strongly suspect that our Jewish "friends," the enemy, who were so anxious to destroy the Jewishness of the Regiment, had their fingers in this Kosher pie!

Now I felt very strongly that unless the Jewish Battalion was treated as such, and all its wants, both physical and spiritual, catered for in a truly Jewish way, this new unit would be an absolute failure, for I could only hope to appeal to them as Jews, and it could hardly be expected that there would be any response to this appeal if I countenanced such an outrage on their religious susceptibilities as forcing them to eat unlawful food. I made such a point of this that I was at length summoned to the War Office by the Adjutant-General, Sir Nevil Macready, who informed me that I was to carry on as if I had an ordinary British battalion, and that there was to be no humbug about Kosher food, or Saturday Sabbaths, or any other such nonsense. I replied very respectfully, but very firmly, that if this was to be the attitude taken up by the War Office, it would be impossible to make the Battalion a success, for the only way to make good Jewish soldiers of the men was by first of all treating them as good Jews; if they were not to be treated as Jews, then I should request to be relieved of my command.

Accordingly, as soon as I returned to Plymouth, I forwarded my resignation, but the G.O.C. Southern Command returned it to me for reconsideration.

In the meantime a telegram was received from the War Office to say that the Kosher food would be granted, and Saturday would be kept as the Sabbath.

After this things went smoothly; Sir Nevil Macready readily lent us his ear when I put up an S.O.S., and, as a matter of fact, he became one of our staunchest friends.

I was more than gratified to receive, a few days later, the following "Kosher" charter from the War Office—a charter which helped us enormously all through our service, not only in England, but also when we got amongst the Philistines in Palestine.

14th Sept., 1917.

20/Gen. No. 4425 (A.G. 2a).
Sir,
With reference to Army Council Instruction 1415 of the 12th Sept., 1917, relating to the formation of Battalions for the reception of Friendly Alien Jews, I am commanded by the Army Council to inform you that, as far as the Military exigencies permit, Saturday should be allowed for their day of rest instead of Sunday.

Arrangements will be made for the provision of Kosher food when possible.

I am, etc.,
(Signed) B. B. Cubitt.

To the General Officer Commanding
in Chief, Southern Command.
O.C. 38th Bn. Royal Fusiliers.

Forwarded for Information.
Devonport, 21/9/17.

(Signed) E. Montagu, Colonel.
A.A. and Q.M.G.

Before we sailed for the front, General Macready did us the honour of coming all the way from London, travelling throughout the night, to pay us a friendly visit, without any of the pomp or circumstance of war, and he was so impressed by what he saw of the soldierly bearing of the men that, from that day until the day he left office, no reasonable request from the Jewish Battalion was ever refused.

I had a final interview with General Macready at the W.O. before setting out for Palestine, when he told me in the presence of Major-General Hutchison, Director of Organization, that the object he aimed at was the formation of a complete Jewish Brigade, and that he was recommending General Allenby to commence that formation as soon as two complete Jewish Battalions arrived in Egypt.

Of course, this was very welcome news to me, because it would mean all the difference in the world to our welfare and comfort if we formed our own Brigade. It would mean that the Brigade would have its own Commander who would be listened to when he represented Jewish things to higher authority. It would mean direct access to the Divisional General, to Ordnance, to supplies, and the hundred and one things which go to make up the efficiency and cater for the comfort of each unit of the Brigade.

No worse fate can befall any Battalion than to be left out by itself in the cold, merely "attached" to a Brigade or a Division, as the case may be. It is nobody's child, and everybody uses it for fatigues and every other kind of dirty work which is hateful to a soldier.

It can be imagined, therefore, how grateful I was to General Macready for promising a Jewish Brigade, for I knew that such a formation would make all the difference in the world to the success of the Jewish cause as a whole and, what was of great importance, to the good name of the Jewish soldier.

CHAPTER VI

WE SET OUT FOR PALESTINE

Towards the end of January, 1918, we were notified that the 38th Battalion was to proceed on Active Service to Palestine. This news was received with great joy by all ranks, and every man was granted ten days' leave to go home and bid farewell to his family.

Of course, our pessimistic friends took every opportunity of maligning the Jew from Russia, and said that the men would desert and we should never see a tenth of them again. I, however, felt otherwise, and had no anxiety about their return. Nor was I disappointed, for when the final roll-call was made there were not so very many absentees, certainly no more than there would have been from an ordinary British battalion, so here again our enemies were confounded and disappointed, for they had hoped for better things.

The Battalion was ordered to concentrate at Southampton for embarkation on the 5th February. Two days before this date Sir

Nevil Macready ordered half the Battalion to come to London to march through the City and East End, before proceeding to Southampton. This march of Jewish soldiers, unique in English military history, proved a brilliant success. The men were quartered in the Tower for the night, and on the morning of the 4th February started from this historic spot, in full kit and with bayonets fixed, preceded by the band of the Coldstream Guards. The blue and white Jewish flag as well as the Union Jack was carried proudly through the City amid cheering crowds. At the Mansion House the Lord Mayor (who had granted us the privilege of marching through the City with fixed bayonets) took the salute, and Sir Nevil Macready was also present to see us march past.

As we approached the Mile End Road the scenes of enthusiasm redoubled, and London's Ghetto fairly rocked with military fervour and roared its welcome to its own. Jewish banners were hung out everywhere, and it certainly was a scene unparalleled in the history of any previous British Battalion. Jabotinsky (who had that day been gazetted to a Lieutenancy in the Battalion) must have rejoiced to see the fruit of all his efforts. After a reception by the Mayor of Stepney, the march was resumed to Camperdown House, where the men were inspected by Sir Francis Lloyd, G.O.C. London District. He complimented them on their smart and soldierly appearance, and made quite an impressive speech, reminding them of the heroism and soldierly qualities of their forefathers, and concluded by saying that he was sure this modern Battalion of Jews now before him would be no whit behind their forbears in covering themselves with military glory.

An excellent lunch was provided for the men in Camperdown House, where speeches were delivered by the Chief Rabbi, the Mayor of Stepney, Mr. Kiley, M.P., Mr. Joseph Cowen (the Chairman), and other friends of the Battalion.

Afterwards the troops proceeded, amid more cheering, to Waterloo, where, before they entrained for Southampton, they were presented by Captain Fredman with a scroll of the law.

My new Adjutant, Captain Leadley, who came to take the place vacated by Captain Neill on promotion to Major, had only just joined us on the morning of our march. He was much surprised at the first Regimental duty he was called upon to perform, which was to take charge, on behalf of the Battalion, of the Scroll of the Law. The excellent Jewish Padre who had just been posted to us, and whose duty this should have been, was with the remainder of the troops at Plymouth.

I was very favourably impressed by Captain Leadley from the first moment I saw him, and during the whole time he remained with the Battalion I never had cause to change my opinion. He was a splendid Adjutant, and, in my opinion, was capable of filling a much higher position on the Army Staff.

When the half Battalion reached Southampton, it joined forces with the other half, which had been brought to that place from Plymouth by Major Ripley, who was now Second-in-Command in place of Major MacDermot, who remained behind with the Depôt. The whole Battalion proceeded to embark on the little steamship Antrim on the 5th February.

Just as Captain Salaman was about to go on board, he was confronted by another Medical Officer, Captain Halden Davis, R.A.M.C., who, at the last moment, was ordered by the War Office to proceed with us instead of Captain Salaman. I knew nothing about this, and was naturally loth to lose Captain Salaman, while he, on his part, was furious at the idea of being left behind. However, there was no help for it, so back he had to go to Plymouth. I think a certain number of the shirkers in the Battalion may have been pleased to see him go, for he stood no nonsense from gentlemen of this kidney.

I had, for some time, been making strenuous efforts to obtain the services of the Rev. L. A. Falk, the Acting Jewish Chaplain at Plymouth, as our spiritual guide, and luckily I was successful, for, at the last moment, all difficulties were surmounted, and he joined us as we embarked. I had had many warnings from people who ought to have known better that he was not a suitable man for the post, but I had seen him and judged for myself, and I felt sure that he would suit my Jews from Russia much better than a Rabbi chosen because he was a Jew from England.

His work and his example to others, during the whole time he served with us, were beyond all praise, and I often felt very glad, when he was put to the test of his manhood, that I had not listened to the voice of the croaker in England.

The embarkation of the Battalion was complete by 5 p.m. on the 5th February, and after dark we steamed out of the harbour and made for Cherbourg. It is fortunate that we escaped enemy submarines, for the little Antrim was packed to its utmost limits, not only with the Jewish Battalion, but also with other troops. We were kept at the British Rest Camp at Cherbourg until the 7th, and then entrained for St. Germain, near Lyons, where we rested from the 9th to the 10th. From here we went on to Faenza, along the beautiful French and Italian Riviera.

The arrangements throughout the journey for feeding the men and giving them hot tea, etc., were not perfect, but on the whole we did not fare badly.

20

We arrived at Faenza on the 13th, and we will always cherish a kindly remembrance of this well-arranged Rest Camp, and of the Staff in charge there. The greatest credit is due to the Commandant, Colonel Scott Harden, for having made a veritable garden in the wilderness, and arranged everything for the comfort and well-being of the tired and travel-stained soldier passing through his capable hands. The only drawback was that my unsophisticated boys were no match for the Scotsmen whom they met in the Sergeant's Mess! However that may be, we all came away with the liveliest feelings of gratitude towards our kindly hosts who had given us a real good time at Faenza.

During our halt at this delightful camp we gave a concert and also a boxing exhibition to the Italian officers of the garrison, both of which were much appreciated. The Italian G.O.C., with all his Staff, also came, and was highly interested in the exhibition. As a special compliment to us, because we were the first complete British Battalion to go through Italy, he reviewed us in front of the Town Hall on our march to the station at 10 o'clock at night.

From Faenza we continued our journey to Taranto, and on the way spent a few pleasant hours at Brindisi. I walked along the docks, and, by the number of naval vessels of all types moored there, I realized that there could not be many Italian warships at sea; but it must be remembered that the Mediterranean was at this time infested with German and Austrian submarines, so that our allies must not be blamed if they were taking as few chances as possible with their ships of war. I remember asking myself the question, what is the use of a ship of war that is afraid to show itself on the open sea?

As we ran along the shores of the Adriatic, we were all wondering whether an Austrian war vessel would not suddenly dash up and blow us and our train to pieces, but, wherever the Austrian fleet may have been that day, fortunately for us it was not cruising on the Adriatic Coast of Italy, and we reached Taranto on the 16th.

Thieving from the trains running through Southern Italy was a pleasant pastime for the natives, but we were fortunate in that we lost but little. We had a couple of accidents during our long railway journey which might, without luck, have proved disastrous. Just before we reached Marseilles a coupling about the middle of the train parted, and the rear carriages were left standing on the line. Fortunately, however, this was discovered before anything serious occurred, and a relief engine brought the stranded portion along. The same thing happened on the Italian railway between Brindisi and Taranto, which delayed us for about eight hours.

The behaviour of the men during the whole long journey of

nine days was exemplary, and I wired a message to this effect to the War Office, for, as Russia was just out of the War, there was some anxiety in England as to how Russian subjects in the British Army would behave on hearing the news.

As a matter of fact recruiting of Russian Jews in England had been stopped after we left Southampton, and many of the men naturally questioned the fairness of the authorities in freeing slackers or late comers, while retaining those who had promptly answered the call.

I cabled this point of view to the Adjutant-General on reaching Taranto and received a reply that all such matters could be settled in Egypt.

We remained basking in the sunshine of Southern Italy for over a week. I met here an old friend of mine, Captain Wake, who had been badly wounded in one of our little wars on the East African coast many years ago. Although minus a leg he was still gallantly doing his bit for England.

We were encamped at Camino, a few miles from Taranto, and our strength at this time was 31 officers, and roughly 900 other ranks.

Two officers and about 70 N.C.O.'s and men sailed on another boat from Marseilles, with the horses, mules and wagons, under the command of Captain Julian, M.C.

While we were at Taranto the Rev. L. A. Falk and I, accompanied by Jabotinsky, searched for and eventually found a suitable Ark in which to place the Scroll of the Law.

At the close of our last Sabbath service before we embarked, I addressed the men, and, pointing to the Ark, told them that while it was with us we need have no fear, that neither submarine nor storm would trouble us, and, therefore, that their minds might be easy on board ship.

We embarked on the Leasoe Castle at 9 o'clock a.m. on the 25th, steamed out of the harbour in the afternoon, under the escort of three Japanese destroyers, and arrived safely in Alexandria on the 28th February, never having seen a submarine or even a ripple on the sea throughout the voyage. Owing to this piece of good luck my reputation as a prophet stood high! It is a curious fact that on her next voyage the Leasoe Castle was torpedoed and sunk.

CHAPTER VII

BACK IN THE LAND OF BONDAGE

When we landed at Alexandria on the 1st March the Battalion was invited by the Jewish community, headed by the Grand Rabbi, to commemorate its safe arrival in Egypt by attending a special service in the beautiful Temple in the street of the Prophet Daniel.

The men got a splendid reception from the Alexandrians as they marched to the Synagogue, where a most impressive service was held, the Grand Rabbi giving the soldiers a special benediction in the grand old language of the Prophets.

After the service, refreshments were served by a number of Jewish ladies, who could hardly indeed believe that they were waiting upon a Battalion, composed of men of their own race, who were now serving as Jewish soldiers under the flag of England. Their faces glowed with joy at the thought that a complete Jewish unit was now before their eyes, and was on its way to assist in releasing the land of their forefathers from the hand of the Turkish oppressor.

It was a great pleasure to meet again those good people who had helped me so wholeheartedly in looking after the wives and dependents of my Zion Mule Corps men who had served in Gallipoli in 1915. Perhaps none worked more zealously or gave more unselfish devotion to those poor and miserable refugees than the Baroness Rosette de Menasce. No matter what I wanted done in the way of help or assistance for the impoverished dependents, I could always rely on this beautiful and charitable lady to see it through.

After lunch was over we marched to the station and entrained for Helmieh, a village a few miles outside Cairo, where the battalion was to be encamped, while completing its training for the front. On arrival there we found awaiting us Captain Julian with the transport section complete, which had safely arrived a couple of days previously.

At Cairo we were met by an emissary from Palestine, who informed us that there was a great Jewish volunteer movement on foot in Judæa, and that hundreds of young men were eager to join the Army, and scores of Jewish ladies were anxious to give their services as nurses, or even as transport drivers.

This was cheering news—news which I naturally thought

would prove most welcome to the Commander-in-Chief of the E.E.F.

The leading Jewish citizens of Cairo, not to be outdone by their brethren of Alexandria, arranged with the authorities, soon after our arrival, that we should attend a religious service in the Chief Synagogue; the battalion had a wonderful reception as it marched through the City, which was thronged with cheering crowds. The High Commissioner, General Sir Francis Reginald Wingate, took the salute as the men marched past the Residency, and evinced the greatest and most friendly interest in this Jewish unit and the Jewish movement generally.

I must mention here that the battalion was much indebted to Mr. Maurice Gattegno, of Cairo, for the immense amount of trouble he took in everything which could be helpful, and the generous way in which he contributed to all our comforts. He had an able helper in his sister-in-law, Miss Viterbo (now Mrs. Hopkin), who was untiring in her efforts on the men's behalf. Mr. Franco and Mr. Cohen, of Alexandria, were also ardent supporters of the battalion.

The Jews who have made Egypt their home are a kindly hospitable people, and we owe them a debt of gratitude for the way they received us and the interest they took in our welfare. The land of the Pharaohs is supposed to eat away the soul of a people and send them after strange gods, but, in my intercourse with the Jews of Egypt, I found that there are to-day many devout men, who work, and pray, and give lavishly of their substance, to the end that Israel may be restored.

The usual infantry training was carried out at Helmieh—drill, physical training, bayonet fighting, bombing, marching, musketry, signalling, etc., went on from morning until night, and the men made excellent progress. In fact, within a few weeks of our arrival in Egypt, no one would have recognized in these bronzed and well set up men, who walked about with a conscious look of pride in themselves and their battalion, the pale, pinched, miserable looking conscripts who joined up at Plymouth.

Soon after our arrival in Egypt I sent the following letter to the Commander-in-Chief:

Cairo,
5th March, 1918.

My dear General,

No doubt you have heard of the arrival of the Jewish Battalion in Egypt. I am very anxious to see you in connection with the formation of a Jewish Brigade, about which the War Office

24

have given me to understand they have made some communication to you.

First of all there will be the position of the Russians to discuss, as I have some hundreds of these with me. They are at present performing their duties cheerfully and well, and I have no fault to find with their attitude; but, as Russia has signed a separate peace, a new situation may arise which I would like to be ready to meet. There are already two more Jewish Battalions formed in England, and one of these, the 39th, was under orders to embark when I left Plymouth. Presumably, it will arrive in Egypt soon. I hear of other battalions for service with the Jewish Brigade being formed in New York; and the Adjutant-General informed me that it was probable that the French authorities would transfer the Polish Jews now serving in France to this Brigade. I am told that there are several hundred young Jews waiting to enlist in Palestine. There are a number more in Cairo and Alexandria.

With your permission I would gladly commence recruiting in these areas, and form a new battalion here. For the purpose of enlisting the Palestine volunteers, it would require a recruiting party to make a trip round the Jewish colonies to collect the recruits. I have an ideal party for such a duty in my present battalion, all speaking Hebrew, headed by an officer who knows Palestine. With your approval I would send this party as soon as possible on tour. Recruiting offices should also be opened in Cairo and Alexandria, where I have promises of every support from the Jewish communities of these cities.

In England the Adjutant-General allowed transfers of Jewish Officers, N.C.O.'s and men. I hope you will be equally indulgent to those who wish to join me from other units now under your command.

I am strongly of the opinion that the training ground of the Jewish Brigade should be in Judæa itself, firstly for its great moral effect on the men; secondly, the climate of Cairo during the training months of March and April will make it practically impossible to do much satisfactory work here. I am convinced that twice the results could be obtained in such a place as Jaffa, or other suitable colony, while the health of the troops would greatly benefit by the cooler climate. It would also enormously stimulate recruiting in Palestine.

I know that the Home Government attach the greatest importance to the moral effect of this Jewish Brigade on the outer world of Jewry—not only in allied and neutral, but also in enemy countries—and such full effect can only be obtained by placing the Brigade in Palestine at the earliest possible moment.

25

There are some other points which I would like to bring to your notice, but I will not add to the length of this letter by mentioning them now.

I should, however, be very glad to see you, and discuss these matters generally with you, and hope you will send instructions for me to report at your headquarters at an early date.

Yours sincerely,
(Signed) J. H. Patterson.

I got a reply from Major-General Louis Jean Bols, the Chief of Staff, asking me to come to G.H.Q., but at the same time informing me that General Allenby was not in favour of my suggestions.

This was somewhat of a surprise to me, for at a time when men were so badly needed, I thought that a Jewish legion, of say 25,000 men, would have been most acceptable on the Palestine front, and, had General Allenby shown himself at all favourable to the idea of a Jewish legion, it would at that time have been an easy task to have obtained any number of men, from America and elsewhere, to fight in Palestine.

Nothing daunted, however, I proceeded to G.H.Q., where I had an interview with the Commander-in-Chief, who told me quite frankly that he was not in sympathy with the War Office policy in sending this Jewish Battalion to Palestine, and that he did not want any further addition such as I suggested to his Forces.

At a subsequent interview which I had with his Chief of Staff, I gathered that I need expect but little sympathy for my battalion, as Major-General Louis Jean Bols told me quite plainly that he was not favourably disposed towards Jewish aspirations.

This anti-Jewish policy of General Allenby and his Chief of Staff came as a shock to me, for I knew that it was the settled intention of His Majesty's Government to support these Jewish Battalions, and the Jewish claim to Palestine, and I had been expecting quite a different reception for my proposals from the E.E.F. authorities to that which they received. I found, to my amazement, that the policy adopted by the Staff towards this Jewish Battalion, and the Jewish problem generally, ran counter to the declared policy of the Home Government. Alas! it seemed that another Pharaoh had arisen who knew not Joseph; and once again we would be expected to make bricks without straw, and become hewers of wood and drawers of water. Instead of this new unit being helped and encouraged, we were, on the contrary, throughout our service in the E.E.F., made to feel that we were merely Ishmaelites, with every hand uplifted against us.

26

I knew full well what our fate would be once the policy of G.H.Q. on this question was known, and, as I will show later, the underlings of the Staff did not fail to play up to the attitude of the higher command. I hoped, however, that the battalion would do such good work that we would eventually overcome all prejudice. We looked for no favours, and only wanted to be treated as a battalion "all out" to do its duty.

The Commander-in-Chief was of course aware by this time of the Arab pretensions to Syria, and as his mind was, no doubt, wholly centred on his own war theatre, he was naturally anxious to placate the Arab at all costs. The Arab was at his door, giving him certain assistance by harrying the Turks to the East of the Jordan, and the fact that the Hedjaz Army was fighting on our side kept Bedouins and other marauders from interfering with our lines of communication—no small matter in Palestine and Syria. The intrusion of the Jew was a disturbing factor to his policy, and was therefore resented.

The local Military Authorities, however, seemed oblivious of the fact that there was a much bigger question involved than that which loomed so largely in their eyes on the Palestine horizon. There was England's world policy to be considered, and her Statesmen had already decided that it was very much in her interests to win over to her side Jewish help and sympathy the world over. Let no one under-estimate what that help meant to the Allies during the Great War. The Jewish element, owing to the Balfour Declaration, came solidly to our side in every land, and in America greatly helped to counter the German propaganda which was fast gripping hold of the United States. It was unfortunate that this far-sighted and wise policy of our Imperial Statesmen was never grasped by their local agents in Palestine.

In the E.E.F., so far as one on the spot could judge, but scant heed was paid to any policy unless it bore on local affairs and coincided with the point of view held by G.H.Q. and the satellites revolving round it.

If only a little wise diplomacy had been employed, I am strongly of the opinion that it would have been quite practicable for the local authorities to have treated the Jewish problem fairly and on the lines of the Balfour Declaration and, at the same time, have retained the Arabs on our side. After all the Arabs were as much interested in the downfall of the Turk as we were ourselves, and, to his honour be it said, the Emir Feisal never showed himself hostile to Jewish aspirations. On the contrary he expressed the utmost goodwill and worked hand in hand with Dr. Weizmann for the common good of both peoples.

The Jew and the Arab are necessary to each other in the Near East, and if England wishes to retain her Empire it is vital to her interests to keep friendly with both. I am afraid that at the moment we are at a discount to the East of Suez. During the stress of war certain promises were made to the Arabs which appear difficult to redeem, mainly due to the policy of France in Syria. I admire France immensely, and that is why I so much deplore her imperialistic aims beyond the Lebanons. She is sowing a rich crop of troubles for herself in these regions, and I am certain that ere long we shall see her reaping a bitter harvest. I met a much travelled French officer in Cairo, who had just relinquished an administrative post in Beyrout, and he told me that, if his Government was wise, it would clear out of Syria, where it would have nothing but trouble for generations to come. "If only," he went on, "England would give us a bit of Africa and take Syria instead, France would make a good bargain."

We, however, do not want Syria, but we do want to see a strong and settled Arab state in these strictly Arab regions, and I sincerely hope that our Statesmen will be wise enough, and energetic enough, to bring about such a desirable consummation. If we permit the Bolshevists and Turks to oust us from our friendship with the Jews and Arabs, and with King Hussein and his son the Emir Feisal (now the King of Irak), upon whom we have alternately blown hot and cold, just as it pleased France to pipe the tune then we shall witness the beginning of the end of our power and prestige in the Orient.

My trip to G.H.Q. was not quite in vain, for just before we left Egypt sanction was given to enlist Palestinian volunteers. I sent to Judæa a specially trained recruiting party, all fluent Hebrew speakers, under the command of Lieutenant Lipsey, to report to Major James de Rothschild of the 39th Battalion, who was the officer appointed to supervise this work in Egypt and Palestine.

The response to Major de Rothschild's appeal was enthusiastic—in fact his chief trouble was to keep out grey-beards and unfledged youths, so eager were all to join up.

Lieutenant Lipsey had some difficulty in keeping his end up in Jerusalem, where there were many anti-Zionists, but finally he worsted his opponents and emerged triumphant with nearly 1,000 recruits.

The following is a translation of the Hebrew recruiting poster sent throughout Palestine at this time:—

Hear, O Israel!

Hear! What does your heart prompt you to do?

28

Shall we not reclaim our heritage and establish its possession
in the eyes of the world?
Hearken! What does your reason say to you?
The British are fighting here before our eyes, and shall
we remain in our houses until they return from the
battle to give us our country which they have redeemed
with their blood?
Hearken! What does your honour and conscience
dictate?
Is it possible for us to accept from the hands of our
righteous redeemers such an offering of blood?
Shall not we too, together with them, offer our lives
for our country?

Hear, O Israel!

The blood of our heroic forefathers, the blood of the
British who fight for us this day, and the blood of
the martyrs, cry unto us from this sacred ground.

Enlist! Enlist!

Shoulder to shoulder, together with our saviours, to the
battle let us go. And salvation is with the Lord.

Be Strong!

CHAPTER VIII

THE FEAST OF THE PASSOVER

At this time G.H.Q. was situated at a place called Bir Salem
(the Well of Peace), ten miles to the east of Jaffa, and as, after my
interview, I had the whole day before me, I borrowed a motor-car
and paid a flying visit to Jerusalem, some thirty miles away to the
eastward. I will not attempt to describe here what I felt as I

approached the Holy City, along the winding road which leads up to it through the rocky Judæan mountains.

I entered the old walled city through the Jaffa Gate, and was soon buried in its gloomy bazaars and labyrinthine passages, seeking out the old historic spots which I had reverenced from the days of my youth. I had but a few hours for my explorations, but they were about the busiest hours I ever spent, and although I have paid many visits to Jerusalem since that date I have not forgotten the glamour thrown over me by my first visit to these sacred shrines and temples of antiquity.

I left Jerusalem at three in the afternoon and was back in my camp at Helmieh within twenty-four hours.

The Battalion was attached to the School of Instruction at Zeitoun (close to Helmieh), which was an unfortunate arrangement, for our requirements were not attended to, and we were often kept idle for long periods owing to want of equipment, such as rifles, etc., to enable the men to fire their musketry course. There was no excuse for this, for there was plenty of equipment of all kinds in the Ordnance Stores at Cairo. It was the fault of the vicious system of having to get everything we wanted through the School of Instruction, whose staff did not seem to think that our requirements needed speeding up. It was not until Brigadier-General A. B. Robertson assumed command of the school that matters were mended, for this officer took a very friendly interest in us and did everything in his power to help us along.

The Feast of the Passover was celebrated during our stay at Helmieh. Thus history was repeating itself in the Land of Bondage in a Jewish Military Camp, after a lapse of over 3,000 years from the date of the original feast.

I had considerable trouble with the authorities in the matter of providing unleavened bread. However, we surmounted all difficulties, and had an exceedingly jovial first night, helped thereto by the excellent Palestinian wine which we received from Mr. Gluskin, the head of the celebrated wine press of Richon-le-Zion, near Jaffa. The unleavened bread for the battalion, during the eight days of the Feast, cost somewhat more than the ordinary ration would have done, so I requested that the excess should be paid for out of Army Funds. This was refused by the local command in Egypt, so I went to the H.Q. Office, where I saw a Jewish Staff Officer, and told him I had come to get this matter adjusted. He said that, as a matter of fact, he had decided against us himself. I told him that I considered his judgment unfair, because the battalion was a Jewish Battalion, and the Army Council had already promised Kosher food whenever it was possible to obtain it, and it would have been a deadly insult to have forced ordinary bread upon the men during Passover. I therefore said that I would appeal against his decision to a higher authority. He replied, "This will do you no good, for you will get the same reply from G.H.Q." He was mistaken, for I found the Gentile, on this particular occasion, more sympathetic than the Jew, and the extra amount was paid by order of the Q.M.G., Sir Walter Campbell.

During our stay at this camp we were reviewed by H.R.H. the Duke of Connaught, and, towards the end of May, by the Commander-in-Chief, General Allenby. Both these officers expressed themselves as pleased with the smart soldierly appearance and steadiness of the men, the Duke of Connaught remarking that "the men all appeared to be triers."

Towards the close of our training at Helmieh, and just as I was beginning to congratulate myself that the battalion was shaping well and would soon be fit for the front, I was staggered by the receipt of a letter from G.H.Q. which aimed a deadly blow at our very existence. It was nothing less than the proposal to break up the battalion and allow the men to join Labour units! This was undoubtedly a clever move on the part of the Staff to rid themselves of the Jewish problem and, at the same time, bring the derision of the world upon the Jew.

It put me in a very difficult position, for I felt very keenly that, if the battalion were disbanded and turned over to Labour units, it would throw an indelible stigma on Jewry.

I felt that it was my duty to protect the battalion from the disgrace that would attach to it if it could be said that the only Jewish unit raised for war purposes had refused to fight—even for Palestine.

I therefore ordered a parade of the men by Companies, and got the officers to point out to the men their sacred duty, and gave instructions for any malcontents to be sent before me for a final appeal. Only twelve men were found who wished to join a Labour unit, and to these twelve (I thought the number appropriate, as it was one for each tribe) I made a strong personal appeal, and after I had pointed out, in the best language at my command, what a stigma they were placing on the battalion, and on their fellow Jews throughout the world, ten saw the error of their ways and cheerfully said they wished to do their duty as soldiers, and continued serving with the battalion, and I am glad to be able to place on record that these ten did very well afterwards in the field, one of them making the supreme sacrifice. Two only remained obdurate to all appeals, and insisted on being posted to a Labour unit, and I think Jewry should remember them to all time. Their names and numbers, and

31

the evil which they did, are recorded in the chronicles of the battalion. They were turned out of the camp and drafted to a Labour unit at a moment's notice, just as if they had been lepers.

Towards the end of April, 1918, we were delighted to welcome the 39th Battalion from England, under the command of Lieut.-Colonel Margolin, D.S.O., and with them as M.O. I was glad to see Captain R. Salaman. We gave the new arrivals a very hearty welcome, the band of the 38th Battalion playing them into Camp amid great enthusiasm.

There was much friendly rivalry between these Jewish Battalions, and honours were about easy in our sporting competitions. We gave one or two "At Homes," to which all Cairo seemed to flock, and I am sure our good Cairene friends were favourably impressed with what they saw of the Jewish Battalions at work and play.

Just about this time we were visited at Helmieh by Dr. Weizmann, Mr. Joseph Cowen, and Mr. Aaronson. All three gave addresses to the men. Mr. Aaronson moved his audience to fury by graphically describing the torture which the Turks had inflicted on his aged father and young sister in Palestine, because they had dared to help England. Mr. Aaronson lived to see his home land freed from the Turk, but soon afterwards lost his life in an aeroplane disaster while crossing from England to France.

Dr. Weizmann has done much and suffered much since he addressed us on that peaceful evening in the Egyptian desert. If he could have foreseen everything I doubt if even his undaunted soul would have faced unblenched all the trials and tribulations which have fallen to his lot since he undertook the arduous task of leading his people back to the Land of Israel. His task has been, if anything, more difficult than was that of the great Lawgiver. The latter had only to surmount the obstinacy of one Pharaoh, while Dr. Weizmann had to overcome that of thousands—not a few of them being Jews!

What a pity it was that the modern leader had not the power to dispense a few of the plagues which Moses eventually found so efficacious. It is a striking testimonial to the genius of Dr. Weizmann that so much has already been accomplished towards the Restoration; the fact that the Jewish people are now within sight of their hearts' desire is, without doubt, mainly due to the patient, persistent, and able diplomacy of this brilliant leader.

It must not be forgotten, however that he was at all times, and often in the teeth of bitter opposition, given the ready help and sympathy of Mr. Lloyd George and Sir Arthur Balfour.

CHAPTER IX

WE SET OUT FOR THE FRONT

By the end of May our training was completed and on the 5th June, 1918, we left Egypt for Palestine, getting a very hearty "send-off" from Col. Margolin and the 39th Battalion.

Before we set out I had the gratification of receiving from General Robertson the following letter:

Savoy Hotel,
Cairo,
4th June, 1918.

Dear Colonel Patterson,

On the eve of your departure for the front I desire to wish you and the officers and men of the 38th Royal Fusiliers God-speed, and success in the tasks which you may be called upon to undertake in the future.

From what I have seen of your battalion I know it will uphold the glorious traditions of the Regiment to which it has the honour to belong, and its career will be watched with interest and sympathy by its well-wishers in all parts of the world.

Personally I am proud to have been associated with the battalion even for a short time.

Its well-known good behaviour must be a source of satisfaction to you, because that will provide a sound foundation on which to build a solid battle discipline, while the progress it made in the training at Helmieh augurs well for its future efficiency.

Yours sincerely,
(Signed) A. B. Robertson.

Lieut.-Col. J. H. Patterson, D.S.O.,
38th Battn., Royal Fusiliers, E.E.F.

The Battalion entrained smoothly and quickly at the railway siding close to our camp and we were soon rolling onward to realize our ideals and aspirations in the Promised Land.

Our Chaplain, who was a man of insight and vision, arranged that our trumpets should sound, and that a short prayer should be said by the troops as they entered, for the first time, the ancient land of their Fathers.

All through the night, as we sped across the Sinai Desert seated in our open trucks, we could see the funnel of the engine belching forth a pillar of flame, and we were greatly reminded of the wanderings of the forefathers of these men in this very Desert, who in their night journeys were always guided by a pillar of fire. Nor did the simile cease as dawn broke, for then the pillar of flame turned into a cloud of smoke shot up into the still morning air.

Soon after sunrise we passed Gaza, the scene of Samson's exploits, and saw, in the distance, the hill to the top of which he carried the gates of the town. Gaza may be considered the bridgehead leading into or out of Egypt. In Biblical times it was always a thorn in the side of the Jews, and they were never able to capture it. It was, however, captured from the Philistines on various occasions both by the Egyptians on their expeditions into Syria and by the Syrians on their expeditions into Egypt. No army could afford to leave it untaken on their lines of communication. It will be remembered that we ourselves made two costly failures here in our first attempts to enter Palestine during the Great War. The third time of course we succeeded, and with its fall the whole plain of Philistia was at our mercy.

As we rolled onward historical places cropped up every few miles and kept us spellbound with interest. Beersheba was away thirty miles to the east, and we hoped in good time to see Dan; meanwhile the Shephelah downs ran parallel to us, ending up with Mount Gezer where David won a victory over the Philistines. This hill was well known to every invading force that has passed through Palestine, and around its base gallant men of many nations have fallen.

In the distance, like a cobalt mist, loomed the mountains of Ephraim and of Judæa, while the "utmost sea" occasionally shimmered on our left.

About noon we steamed through a grove of olives into Ludd (the ancient Lydda), where we detrained. It was one of the hottest days I have ever experienced, and our march to Surafend, under a blazing midday midsummer sun, loaded up as we were with full kit, was a severe test of the endurance of the men.

Almost as soon as we reached our bivouac at Surafend the Jewish Colonists of Richon-le-Zion, Jaffa, Rechoboth and all the surrounding colonies came out in their hundreds with flags and banners, on foot, on horseback, and in chariots, to greet us, and show us how much they thought of their brethren who had come all the way from England to help them to redeem their country.

34

Amongst the Zionists from Jaffa and Richon-le-Zion were many scores of both men and women who had already volunteered for service with the Army.

It was an inspiring sight to see how these young men and women rode and managed their horses. No cowboy of the Western States of America could be more expert. It is quite evident that a new and free Jewish race is arising among the colonists of Palestine, for even the small children of eight and nine years of age can ride and manage horses with ease. We celebrated our first Sabbath in Palestine at Surafend, where special prayers for the occasion were recited, including one composed by the Haham Bashi of Egypt, Rabbi Simeon.

Richon-le-Zion, besides sending its quota of young men and women to greet us, sent us also three casks of choice Richon wine, which in those thirsty days the battalion much appreciated.

We remained at Surafend for three days, and during our stay there, were inspected in our bivouac by General Allenby, who again expressed himself as well pleased with all he saw.

Major James de Rothschild came over from Jaffa, where he was then doing recruiting duty, and gave us a God-speed as we left our pleasant surroundings at Surafend for our journey to the Front.

We marched off at 3 o'clock on the afternoon of the 9th June, and reached El Kubab at 8.15 the same evening. Personally I only went half-way, for I was recalled to Cairo to preside at a General Court-Martial assembled there for the trial of three Royal Air Force officers who had been performing some unauthorised stunts. I rejoined the Battalion at Umm Suffah, a few miles short of the Turkish lines. While the 38th was at this place there was an air raid on our lines, but no damage was done.

From El Kubab the Battalion went to Beit Nuba. They left on the 11th, and reached Harith the same day, where they came under the orders of Brigadier-General E. M. Morris, a first-rate soldier commanding the 10th Irish Division. They marched out of Harith at 5 p.m. on the 12th, and arrived at Umm Suffah at 10 p.m. the same day.

We were now among the hills of Samaria and the transport was much delayed on this march owing to the frightfully rough and stony road. Several wheels got broken and, as a matter of fact, the transport, with the food, etc., did not arrive until the early morning of the 13th.

On the 13th June the Battalion was placed in Divisional Reserve. On Saturday the 15th it first came under shell fire while we were holding Divine Service. Shells exploded quite close to the men,

35

but no damage was done, and the battalion took its baptism of fire quite cheerfully.

During the week that followed the Companies were posted to units already in the line, to gain some knowledge of the country, and to learn the nature of the duties to be carried out in the fighting zone.

Before we took our place in the line we were inspected by the G.O.C. 10th Division, who, when the inspection was over, expressed himself as very pleased with the general appearance and steadiness of the men.

On the 27th June A, B, and C Companies were detailed to garrison supporting points on the front occupied by the 31st Infantry Brigade, to which we were now attached, and which was under the command of Brigadier-General W. B. Emery, a genial gunner.

Battalion Headquarters and D Company moved up to the front on the 30th June and took over the second line of supporting points, from a place known as the Wadi Tiyur to the Wadi Belat, just to the west of the main road running from Jerusalem to Nablus (the ancient Shechem), where it cuts the Wadi Jib some twenty miles north of the Holy City.

On the 3rd July the Battalion relieved 2/101 Grenadiers in the left sector of the 31st Infantry Brigade front, the relief being commenced after dark and completed by 10.15 p.m.

We found the piece of country we took over most interesting. We occupied the summits of the hills facing the Turkish position, and were responsible for some three or four miles of front.

Our right rested upon Jiljilia, a pretty hamlet of Samaria, and our left upon Abwein, a strong, stone-built Arab village, nestling half-way down a steep hillside, surrounded by fig and olive trees. Our line on the hills between these two places twisted and turned about like a snake, for of course we conformed to the nature of the ground. Our frontage towards the enemy descended into the valley, some 200 feet below, in a series of rocky terraces, each having a drop of from six to twenty feet. These terraces and hill slopes were dotted with olive trees. A wadi, called the Wadi Gharib, ran through the narrow valley which lay at the bottom, and then there was a very steep ascent up the opposite side to the Turkish line.

Our front wire was actually a few hundred yards down over the crest of the hill on the Turkish side, for from this position we had a better field of fire.

When we took over this position from Lieut.-Colonel Strong, the O.C. of the 2/101 Grenadiers, a considerable amount of work necessarily remained to be done, building stone sangars, digging trenches, making roadways, and generally improving the position in every possible way.

Our line was divided into four sections, one company guarding each part, Major Neill on the extreme right holding Jiljilia, and Captain Brown with his Company in Abwein.

We at once assumed a vigorous offensive policy; our patrols were pushed out every night down into the valley, and often up to the Turkish wire on the opposite hills. During daylight only the Observation Posts were manned along our front wire. A couple of men in each vantage point, equipped with field glasses or telescopes, and provided with a telephone, kept us informed of any movement in the Turkish lines. As soon as darkness had fallen each company marched its men over the crest of the hills and took up position in the sangars and defence posts along the barbed wire fence. All night long work and building, etc., went on, the unfortunate men getting very little rest. Listening posts were established well out beyond the wire, and strong patrols went down the ledges looking for trouble in Turkish territory. Our aggressive policy thoroughly scared the Turks, so much so that they never once attempted to come anywhere near our front.

Just as dawn was breaking, having made certain by means of patrols and scouts that no Turks were in the neighbourhood, the troops returned to their bivouacs behind the crest, leaving only the Observation Posts on the watch.

I had a very good Intelligence Officer in Lieutenant Simon Abrahams, who explored "no man's land" very methodically, and who earned a high measure of praise from our Brigade Commander. Abrahams would go out with a daring scout like Pte. Angel (who afterwards won the M.C.) and sketch roads, routes, tracks, etc., right under the very noses of the Turks, and so careful was he, and so secretive, that his presence on the debatable ground was never even suspected by the enemy.

It might be thought that when the men had finished their night's vigil they would be allowed to rest, but instead of this, as soon as a hasty breakfast had been swallowed, they immediately had to fix up barbed wire entanglements, build stonework redoubts, gun emplacements, make railways down the hills, or bury animals which had died or been killed in somebody else's camp.

Anything and everything was demanded from the battalion, and every call, no matter how distasteful, was responded to with readiness, if not with cheerfulness. All the time we were holding this bit of the Nablus front, from the Wadi Jib to the Wadi Gharib, the men were constantly running about on arduous jobs and as busy as bees.

About this time there was a rumour that we were soon to take the offensive, and I was especially pleased when I got a confidential communication from our Brigade Commander ordering me to prepare a careful reconnaissance of the country to our left front, where the surprise attack on the Turks was to be made. A good track up to the enemy wire, concealed as much as possible from his view, had to be found, the general idea being that once there we would make a sweep to the right along the Turkish front opposed to our lines. I detailed Captain T. B. Brown for this important task, which he carried out admirably. A suitable route by which to return with the expected prisoners and loot had also to be discovered and sketched, and Lieutenant Simon Abrahams was in his element when I selected him for this adventure.

The hope of coming to grips with the Turks buoyed us up considerably, and the prospect of a battle in which we felt sure we would do well helped us through the trying and weary round of daily routine.

Our Brigadier was a soldier whom we all liked, but he had a mania for putting up barbed-wire fences, and at last we erected so much on our front that we caused a serious shortage of this material in the E.E.F., and further wiring was prohibited.

On the 10th July our Transport was shelled. Luckily only one mule was killed and one wounded.

We were heavily bombarded by guns of various calibres at 2.30 in the morning on July 14th, but it was an absolute waste on the part of the Turks, for not a single casualty of any kind was sustained.

On this day the Turks and Germans attacked in the Jordan Valley and got severely mauled by the Anzac Mounted Division. We, too, expected an attack, but soon after dawn the shelling ceased and the situation became normal.

While the Battalion was holding the forward trenches I always made a round of the posts every night to see that every one was on the alert and that they knew what to do in case of attack.

I made the men place white stones along the wire so that they could take aim on them in case of a Turkish assault in the dark, and arranged bombing parties at various points; in fact, we were all ready to give the enemy a very warm reception if he ever came our way.

Once, on going my rounds, I heard a noise a little way down the hill, so I ordered a young soldier to throw a bomb; he failed to get the pin quite out and slipped the "dud" into his great-coat pocket; fortunately, a sergeant standing near saw what had happened and, on examining the "dud," found the pin practically released! The slightest movements would have set the bomb off and we should all have been blown sky high.

No matter at what hour I returned from my tour of inspection along the battle line, I always found my faithful orderly, Corporal Hutchinson, awaiting me with a "nightcap" such as could only be mixed by the dexterous hand of an old campaigner. Hutchinson served with me when I commanded a battalion of the Irish Fusiliers, and followed my fortunes when I went to command the Dublin Fusiliers. On asking him if he would go with me to the Jewish Battalion, he replied, "Oh, be the hokey!—but shure, Sir, that's where you'll be wanting me the most."

Hutchinson remained with me until we set out for the Jordan Valley, when he was taken ill and invalided home. I missed him sadly, for he used to remain by my tent door and ward off any undesirable intruder like a well-trained watch dog. A more faithful, loyal and trust-worthy soldier never shouldered a rifle.

CHAPTER X

THE NABLUS FRONT

On the 17th July we were transferred to the 60th Division and attached to one of its Brigades.

We were very sorry to leave the 10th Division, for we had made many good friends all round, and our Divisional and Brigade Commanders had always treated us fairly and justly.

On the evil day of our transfer a fatal accident befell Lieutenant B. Wolffe. He was in charge of the transport wagons and was engaged in loading up supplies at the Ordnance Depôt. The drivers were, of course, dismounted and standing by their teams while the work of loading was going ahead. A sudden noise frightened one of the teams, and off the four horses careered at a mad gallop. They were heading straight for some troops standing near, and Lieutenant Wolffe, seeing this, made a gallant attempt to stop them by springing at the heads of the leaders as they dashed past. Unfortunately they were going too fast for him, and he was dragged under their feet, the wagon passing over his body.

I visited him in hospital, as did also our Chaplain and others, and we cheered him up as much as possible, but he died on the 20th, and his death cast a gloom over the whole battalion, for he was a most conscientious officer, a good Jew, and well liked by all ranks. He was buried with full Jewish rites, a "Minyan" from the battalion attending.

The Commander-in-Chief in General Orders eulogised the gallant attempt which he made when he sacrificed his own life in his plucky effort to save others.

On the 24th July I was requested by Dr. Weizmann to bring a representative party of officers and men of the battalion to a most interesting ceremony at Jerusalem—the laying of the foundation stones of the Hebrew University On Mount Scopus.

In the days of her past greatness the law was expounded at Jerusalem. It is quite possible that again, even in our own days, we shall hear a message of peace and goodwill issue forth from the Temple of Learning overlooking the Holy City.

The site chosen for the building is a magnificent one. It looks down on the domes and minarets of Jerusalem on the one side, and, on the other, overlooks the Jordan Valley and the Dead Sea, with the green hills of Moab looming in the distance.

The ceremony itself was a most interesting one. The Commander-in-Chief was present; also all the civil and religious heads of the Jewish, Christian, and Moslem communities, while a vast multitude of people of all creeds thronged along the slopes of Scopus from Jerusalem—a seemingly good omen for future peace and concord. It was a truly inspiring and historic occasion, and augured well for the future greatness of the University. Stones were laid by the Christian Bishop in Jerusalem and by the Mufti (the Chief Mohammedan dignitary). One was also laid by Dr. Weizmann in the name of the Jewish Regiment, while what perhaps appealed to me most of all was the part taken by Jewish children in laying a stone representing the Hope of Israel.

On my return to the Battalion I found the Headquarters encamped in a pretty grove of olives on the Inniskilling Road, some two miles behind the firing line. While we were here our Chaplain, the Rev. L. A. Falk, one day discovered a red granite column embedded in the side of a hill. This we unearthed and, on measuring it, found that it was about 12 feet high and about 2 feet in diameter. We erected it in our camp in a grove of olive trees. I much perturbed our good Rabbi by chaffingly suggesting to him that we had been erecting an altar to Baal, in a grove, in one of the high places! Our find got noised abroad, and the Governor of Jerusalem, Colonel Storrs, with his assistant, Lord William Percy, motored out from Jerusalem to see it. They had lunch with us, and I was delighted to note that Lord William Percy took a keen interest in preserving the fauna of Palestine, and had induced General Allenby to impose strict limitations on the shooting of birds and beasts.

Our transfer to the 60th Division did not, for the time at least, result in any change in our position in the line, but, almost from the moment we joined the new Brigade, we felt the hostility shown towards all things Jewish by the Brigade Commander. I endeavoured to counter his prejudice against the battalion, during a friendly after-dinner chat, by pointing out the immense debt we owed to the "People of the Book" for all they have done towards civilising and humanizing the world for thousands of years. During their struggle for existence through centuries of exile, in countries where every form of torture and repression had been in vogue against them, they never lost their age-long Hope of a Restoration. The General seemed, like many others, to have a very vague idea as to the aim of the Zionists, which is simply to establish a National Home in Palestine where Jewish life, rooted in its own soil, would have an opportunity of developing on modern lines, in accordance with its own ideals. I gave the Brigadier some new ideas on Jews, but all my eloquence was in vain, for I failed to convert him, and he hinted that I was only wasting my time by being mixed up with a Jewish unit!

But although the Brigadier was right in one way when he said "You will get nothing out of it," yet in another way he was altogether wrong, for I have got a very great deal out of my service with this Jewish Battalion. I have had the satisfaction of proving that, in spite of all obstacles placed in its path, this new unit showed that it was worthy of the best traditions of the Maccabæans, those doughty Jewish soldiers who, on many a well-fought field, defeated the legions of Antiochus and freed Judæa from a foreign yoke.

But it is not by fighting alone that a good battalion is proved, and the Jewish unit was tested in many ways as this record will show.

There was no respite from such work as digging trenches, building stone sangars, and constructing roads along the hill-sides, by day and by night; nevertheless, every soldierly duty allotted was carried out cheerfully and promptly.

The rumour which had got abroad about the attack on the Turkish trenches opposite our front now crystallised into definite shape, and the actual date of the attack was often hinted at.

A few days before the assault was to take place our Brigadier gave us the special job of making stone emplacements, almost within sight of the Turks, just above the village of Jiljilia, and as we fondly hoped we would have a place in the assaulting column, all hands worked with a will, especially our two Christian Lithuanians, Stenelus and Sterilitis; these men amazed the British gunners by the ease with which they placed huge blocks of stone in position—all done by sheer strength of muscle combined with hearty good will.

This particular piece of work was under the supervision of Major Neill, and, as it had to be done in record time, his task was no easy one, but, fortunately for him and his Company, the Turks never spotted what was going on, and before we left these parts Major Neill saw the guns safely emplaced without suffering a single casualty.

All this stone work on the steep sides of a hill, coupled with heavy marching to and fro, and scrambling up and down, was not good for the men's clothing, which soon got worn, ragged and dirty. A false step on a slippery slope meant that the seat of a man's flimsy shorts was rent asunder, and it was quite usual to see the tail of a shirt hanging out! Yet, no matter how ragged and disreputable-looking the men were, I found it impossible to get any renewal of clothing, although it was freely handed out to other units.

It seemed as if it were a joy to some people to be able to withhold necessary articles of clothing, such as shirts, boots, socks, shorts, etc., and keep the men working on dirty jobs, and then say with glee, "Look at the ragged dirty Jews."

It must be remembered that we could not obtain enough water even to wash our faces, for every drop had to be carried up the precipitous sides of the hills on camels as far as they could clamber, and then by mules and donkeys up the steeper parts. Often there was a shortage of the precious fluid even for tea-making.

I wrote urgent letters again and again, and protested that the men were unfit to march for want of shoes, and that many of them were actually exposing their nakedness for want of clothing. I sent my Quartermaster, Lieutenant Smythe, day after day, to the Ordnance Stores trying to extract necessary articles, but all in vain! We were nobody's children, and consequently we could get nothing. I saw the Brigadier, and represented to him that in many cases our men were ragged, shirtless, sockless, and bootless, but if he made any representations on our behalf there was no result.

Had we belonged to a Brigade instead of being merely "attached" most of our troubles would never have arisen, but the policy adopted by the local Staff was to keep us as "wandering Jews," pitched from one Brigade to another, in a continuous round of General Post.

It was a heart-breaking experience as any soldier will understand.

42

At last I rode over to my old Gallipoli friend, Colonel O'Hara, who was on the Staff of the 10th Division, and he, like the good soldier that he is, helped me out of my difficulty as far as it lay in his power.

What a difference it makes when one meets a good Staff Officer! Not nearly enough care is given to the task of selecting the right men for this all-important branch of the Army. They are too often selected for any reason except the right one, viz., efficiency.

The Brigade to which we were attached was fortunate in having at least one good Staff Officer. The Brigade Major was a thoroughly capable soldier, and always out to help in every way in his power.

The Brigadier often caused me much inward amusement by pointedly appealing in my presence to the judgment of a certain Colonel X, an officer junior to me, who was in command of a section on our right. If I had a sangar built which commanded a good field of fire, it was sure to be found fault with, and another had to be built in a site chosen by their joint wisdom.

One night the gallant Brigadier came across the spot where I had my outlook post established; he thought it was in the wrong place, of course, and consulted his friend, Colonel X, as to where it should be.

"Don't you think it ought to be on the top of this house?" said the General. The Colonel climbed to the top of the house, gazed round in the inky darkness, came down again, and said he quite agreed with the General, as all good, well-trained Colonels, with an eye to the main chance, invariably do!

I was then ordered to put the outlook on the top of the house, which had a flat roof, where a man would be seen by every Turk for miles round! Needless to say, I never placed an observer in this absurd position.

Just about this time one of my men, quite a youth, was found asleep at his post, and as this is about the most serious crime of which a sentry can be guilty, he was tried by General Court Martial and sentenced to death.

A few days later a telegram came from the Provost Marshal ordering me to send the condemned man under strong escort, with two senior non-commissioned officers, to the prisoners' compound some distance away. I feared that the unfortunate lad would be shot at dawn, and as I knew he had been working exceedingly hard, day and night, for 48 hours before he was found asleep at his post, and was of good character and very young, I determined to try to save him. I therefore sent a private wire to General Allenby asking him on these grounds to reprieve him.

My friend the Brigadier saw the wire before it was despatched and stopped it. However, one of my men in the Signal Office told me of this, so I immediately wrote a confidential letter to General Allenby, gave it to a motor-cyclist, and sent him off post haste to G.H.Q., some thirty miles away, telling him to ride for all he was worth, as a man's life hung on his speed.

I am glad to say that not only did General Allenby reprieve the man and reduce the sentence to a certain number of years' imprisonment, but he suspended even that punishment, provided the man proved himself worthy of forgiveness by doing his duty faithfully in the battalion.

The young soldier returned to us overjoyed and full of gratitude for his release. He proved himself worthy in every respect, and was never afterwards called upon to do a day's imprisonment.

Not satisfied with having held up the wire, the Brigadier motored some miles away to report the matter to the Divisional General, Sir John Shea.

I was duly haled before the General, not knowing for what reason, until he said, "You know you will get yourself into trouble if you go sending telegrams direct to the Commander-in-Chief." It then dawned on me for the first time why I had been sent for.

I explained all the circumstances to the General, and said that, in such an emergency, I felt justified in what I had done. Besides, I said, I had not addressed the Commander-in-Chief as such, but as General Allenby, an officer whom I had known for many years. I also confessed that, when I found that the wire had been blocked, I had immediately written a letter of appeal to General Allenby, and had sent it off by a special cyclist despatch rider.

The General pretended to be so horrified at this that he needed a cocktail to revive him—in which I may add he asked me to join him. I do not know what he thought of the Brigadier's action, but I can leave the reader to imagine what I thought of it!

A few days later, when I was breakfasting with General Shea, I was much amused when he told me that when he was at home his children insisted on his reading a lion story to them every evening out of "The Man-Eaters of Tsavo"!

From the frequent consultations between the Brigadier and his friend Colonel X I felt that something was on foot, but little realised that it was a matter which, if carried out, would strike a blow at the very identity of the Jewish Battalions. This, however, soon became evident.

Shortly after my interview with the Divisional General I was called to the telephone to speak to the Brigadier, who said, apparently with great satisfaction, "I want to tell you that your

Battalion and the 39th Battalion (which was then on its way up from Egypt) are to be brigaded with two West Indian Battalions, and you are to be placed under the command of Colonel X, who is now a General and has come to live near my camp. You will find General X a very nice man." I thanked the Brigadier for his interesting information and hung up the receiver.

It was now clearly my duty to stop this second attempt to destroy the identity of the Jewish Battalions in Palestine or resign my command. It was no easy task to achieve, because our good friends had worked underground all the time, and sprang this surprise upon me only when it became an accomplished fact; Colonel X had actually been appointed to the command, a Brigade Major and a Staff Captain had been posted to the new Brigade, while the transport and ordnance section of the formation had been already organized and sent to Jericho.

The Staff at G.H.Q. had, of course, arranged the whole affair, and it would be no easy task to get the Commander-in-Chief to countermand the Brigade formation. I felt that a very firm stand must be taken if this blow aimed at Jewish prestige was to be averted.

I accordingly wrote a strong letter direct to General Allenby, pointing out that, if such a scheme were carried out, it would involve very grave issues. The Adjutant-General at the War Office had promised that the Jewish Battalions would be formed into a Jewish Brigade, and to depart from this declared policy would be looked upon as a direct slight, both by the Jewish Battalions and by Jewry the world over. Loth as I was to worry the Commander-in-Chief, I considered it my duty to him, to my men, to myself, and to Jewry to see that Jewish interests were not trampled upon without a protest while I retained command. I requested therefore that the orders should be cancelled, and, if not, that I should be relieved of my command.

That my attitude on this question was correct was proved by the receipt of a most friendly reply from General Allenby, in which he thanked me for my letter and said:

I see the undesirability of brigading Jewish with West Indian Battalions, and I have decided not to do so. I shall form a provisional Brigade of the two Jewish Battalions until a complete Jewish Brigade can be formed, and they will be under you.

The whole tone of this letter showed that the C.-in-C. had been badly advised by his Staff in this attempted amalgamation of the Jewish with the West Indian Battalions.

45

A few hours after I had received General Allenby's communication a wire came from G.H.Q. cancelling all the orders which had already been issued with regard to the formation of the new Brigade.

Thus I won the second round in my fight for fair play for the Jewish Battalions and Jewish ideals generally.

I realized that my stand for justice would be bitterly resented by certain individuals at G.H.Q., and that, sooner or later, I would be penalised for having upset their attempted little coup.

CHAPTER XI

WE MARCH TO THE JORDAN VALLEY

Within two days of the receipt of General Allenby's letter cancelling the mixed Brigade formation, we were suddenly ordered to leave the cool and pleasant hill-tops of Ephraim and march down to the sweltering heat and fever-stricken desolation of the Jordan Valley, 1,300 feet below sea level, in the very hottest and most unhealthy month of the year.

We, of course, took our orders for the deadly Valley quite cheerfully, feeling that it was "not ours to reason why," but we did feel that it was a blow below the belt to be taken out of the line on the Nablus front, just as an attack, for which we had done most of the spade work, was about to be made.

Had we remained with General Emery, I feel sure that he would have given us a chance to show our mettle in the raid which was timed to take place on 12th August, 1918.

Even when we were transferred to the Brigade in the 60th Division we still looked forward to taking part in this move, and, as I have already mentioned, we slaved away at every kind of preparation for the affair, but, alas, we were taken out of the line, and ordered to march to a new front, just three days before the attack.

It almost looked as if our enemies feared we would do well, and our prowess would then get noised abroad to the discomfiture of our detractors.

On the 9th August we marched from our pretty camp at Inniskilling Road, where we had revelled in the grateful shade of the olive trees which abound there, and took the road, bag and baggage, for Ram Allah, our first halt, where we were to bivouac. Here we were to get further orders from the G.O.C. 53rd Division, whose headquarters were in that ancient town. It was midnight when we got to our camp, where we found that someone had carefully chosen a site for us which was literally one mass of stones. It must have been the favourite place of execution in olden days when stoning to death was in vogue, and the stones had never since been gathered up! There was no grumbling, however; every man cleared a little patch whereon to lie down on his waterproof sheet, and slept the sleep of the tired. We remained at this delectable spot for the best part of two days, and on the afternoon of the 11th we marched to Jerusalem, where we came under the orders of the Desert Mounted Corps.

We bivouacked about a mile or so short of Jerusalem, and, as the camp was reached long after dark, the City remained hidden until dawn next morning. I had a cheery and welcome dinner the evening we arrived with Lieutenant-General Sir Philip Chetwode, who commanded the 20th Corps, at his headquarters at the German Hospice on the Mount of Olives.

I was awake about 5 o'clock next morning, just as the mist was beginning to disperse, and woke up everybody all round about me to have their first look at the Holy City. My officers were all very tired, so merely gave one peep at it out of sleepy eyes, and then buried themselves once more in their blankets. Later on the men spent the whole of the forenoon visiting Jerusalem, and especially the celebrated Wailing Wall, which is the only authentic portion of the Temple enclosure which still remains. Its huge blocks of stone seem to be as indestructible as the indomitable race which designed, shaped, and placed them in position so many centuries ago. The Jewish "bevel" is a noticeable feature in the stones. Here the Jews for nearly two thousand years have wept and wailed, placing their foreheads against the walls and copiously watering the masonry with their tears. The wailing of the Jews at this remnant of their Temple is one of the most pathetic and curious sights I have ever witnessed.

The Jewish mendicants who are allowed to congregate in the vicinity of the Wailing Wall are not a pleasing spectacle, and I hope that one of the first acts of the Zionists will be the removal of this blot on Jewry.

Bethlehem can be reached in a few minutes by motor from

47

Jerusalem, and near to it Rachel's tomb stands by the roadside, while almost opposite is the field in which Ruth gleaned.

At 4.30 in the afternoon of this day (12th August) we marched off under the walls of Jerusalem, past the Damascus Gate, skirted the Garden of Gethsemane, and wended our way on to the road which would take us down to Jericho. It was a lovely sight as we halted and looked back over the Valley of Jehoshaphat, with the brook Kidron between us and the walls of the venerable city, the beautiful Mosque of Omar overshadowing the Temple area, the mysterious Golden Gates fronting us, sealed up, and the westering sun gilding Mount Zion.

I have seen Jerusalem since from many points, but the view from the corner of the Jericho Road, where it skirts the Mount of Olives on the descent to Bethany, is, to my mind, by far the most beautiful and impressive. I halted every platoon there, so that all might look well at the glory of it—a glory which, alas, some of them would never again return to look upon.

We bivouacked about three miles beyond Jerusalem, and next morning (13th August) marched through Bethany while it was yet dark, and reached our bivouac at Talaat ed Dumm at 2.30 in the afternoon. I reported our arrival to General Chauvel, of the Australian Mounted Division, whose headquarters were at this place, and from his hut I had a splendid view of the beauty and desolation of the Jordan Valley which lay spread out before me.

Talaat ed Dumm is a weird uncanny spot. It is mentioned in the Book of Joshua as Adummim, and is the gate of the Judæan wilderness. The red and yellow barren hills and rocky narrow valleys have a peculiar desolation all their own, while the heat at the time we were there was scorching.

By some jugglery on the part of the Staff, all our transport animals had been taken away from us, and we found ourselves stranded without a particle of shade, shelter, or food on this God-forsaken spot, sweltering in the fierce rays of the burning sun. At last, towards sundown, our baggage and rations arrived in motor lorries, dinners and teas were rolled into one, and peace reigned once more in this drowsy wilderness.

When the terrific heat had become somewhat less scorching, accompanied by the Padre, I wandered up to an ancient ruin which topped the summit of a hill dominating the roadway. This proved to be the castle of a redoubtable robber chief, who had lived here in bygone days and taken his toll from every traveller. From time immemorial this had been the stronghold of the robber bands who waylaid, robbed, and even murdered those journeying to and fro between Jerusalem and Jericho. It was close to this bandit's castle

48

that the Good Samaritan poured oil and wine into the wounds of the unfortunate wayfarer who had fallen among thieves. It was an ideal spot for a robber's lair, because it commands a full view of what is practically the only route for caravans through this dreary barren wilderness.

We were not sorry to leave our camp at dawn, and strode out so merrily that we overtook a Cavalry Brigade which blocked our way! As we marched down the steep descent to the Jordan Valley we had on our left the Wadi Kelt, which wound its tortuous course through the boulders at the bottom, hundreds of feet sheer below us. Some people say that it was here that the Prophet Elijah was fed by the ravens, but it has been satisfactorily proved that the brook Cherith, where Elijah hid, is now known as the Wadi Fusail. It runs into the Jordan from the westward, near a place called the rock of Oreb.

This suggested an idea to me that the "ravens" spoken of in the Bible were not birds but people, for the word "Oreb" means a raven. Now we know there was a prince called Oreb, for we have an account of his death in Judges, Chapter 7, Verse 25. It is also a well-known fact that in the East tribes take their names from their prince or chief man, so that in all probability there was a tribe called Orbim (the plural of "oreb" or raven).

The place where Prince Oreb was slain was the rock of Oreb, and it is known to this day as "Tel el Orbaim." Moreover, this place is in Gilead, which was Elijah's old home, so it was quite natural that he should flee to this neighbourhood and be fed with flesh and bread, night and morning, by his friends the Orbim, or "Ravens."

How similar, too, are the words used in the 4th and 9th verses of 1st Kings, Chapter 17: "I have commanded the ravens to feed thee there," and "I have commanded a widow woman there to sustain thee!"

Can it be possible that the ravens were people and not birds, and that our old and learned translators fell into the error of thinking that they were birds, because they did not know of the possible existence of a tribe called "Orbim" or "Ravens"?

We continued our march down through the Judæan wilderness, the place where the High Priest yearly turned loose the Scapegoat which bore on its head the sins of the Children of Israel.

Occasionally, away to our right, between the desolate, dusty, sulphurous-looking hills, we caught a momentary glimpse of the emerald sheen of the Dead Sea, while away on our left on the edge of the valley, stood out the Mount of Temptation.

The moment we got down to the Jordan Valley (or Ghor, as the Arabs call it) the real trials of the men began. The heat was

49

intense, and the going became very heavy, for we had no longer a good metalled road on which to march. Dust lay a foot deep on the path; it was exceedingly fine and looked like the best powdered cement. As the men marched clouds of it arose and choked them, while their feet were actually sucked down at each step, and an effort had to be made to draw the foot out again, as if some devil were below, pulling at the sole of the boot.

The sixteen platoons forming the battalion marched well apart in order to evade as much of this blinding, choking, sulphurous dust as possible.

Jericho, the city of the Palms, lay a little to our right. We passed its outskirts and halted for a rest under Old Jericho, the walls of which the Bible tells us miraculously fell to Joshua's trumpets over 3,000 years ago. This was a thought which acted as a spur to every Jewish soldier, and although the march was a hard one and the worst of it had yet to be done, the men came through the ordeal triumphantly, and very few dropped out by the way. Those who did fall by the wayside were helped along by our Padre, the Rev. L. A. Falk, who gave up his horse to the footsore and carried the pack and rifle of the weary, thus cheering them along into Camp. This time it was the Priest who proved the Good Samaritan on the road to Jericho.

Soon after we recommenced our march from under the walls of old Jericho a huge black column of fine dust, whose top was lost in the Heavens, arose in front of us and gyrated slowly and gracefully as our vanguard, leading us onward to our bivouac on the banks of a cool and pleasant brook, where it vanished. I felt that this was a good omen for our success in the Jordan Valley, for it was a case of the Children of Israel being led once more by a pillar of cloud.

The Headquarters of the Australian Mounted Division was close beside our bivouac, and here I had a very welcome breakfast with Major-General H. W. Hodgson, its capable and genial Commander. The General told me that he would review the battalion on the following afternoon, on its march out to the new camping ground on the Auja.

Next morning, while the men were resting and refreshing themselves on the banks of the Nueiameh (for so the cool stream was named), I rode down the Valley to the eastward of Jericho, accompanied by our Padre.

We waded through the Wadi Kelt, luxuriant grass growing where the water had overflowed its banks, showing how fruitful the Valley would be if it were irrigated. We searched the plain to discover, if possible, some traces of the ancient Gilgal, Joshua's

50

G.H.Q., and eventually we came upon what we took to be the site, some three miles to the south-east of Old Jericho. At all events we found some very ancient stonework buried in grass-grown mounds just about where Gilgal might be looked for, and I feel sure that if excavations were carried out here some very interesting discoveries would be made.

After we had briefly examined the ruins, I suggested to the Padre that we should go and breakfast in Jericho, if indeed we could find a caravanserai there, so in search of a hostelry we rode into the modern city of the Palms.

It proved to be but a poor tumble-down jumble of buildings, as might have been expected. However, as we rode along, we came upon a somewhat pretentious looking building on which was painted "The Gilgal Hotel." Whatever doubt there may have been about the ancient Gilgal, here at any rate was a modern one, the discovery of which at this moment was most opportune, for we were both decidedly hungry after our explorations.

As we rode into the courtyard a dozen Arab urchins who had been lounging about made a dash for our horses, each eager to grasp the reins in the hope of some "baksheesh." An elderly dame, on hearing the scuffle, emerged from a doorway, scattered the surplus boys, and called loudly, "Victoria, Victoria." A musical voice from a room above responded to this familiar name, and, on looking up, we saw a buxom, olive-tinted damsel step on to the balcony. A voluble dialogue then took place between mother and daughter, the result of which was that Victoria, in excellent English, invited us up to breakfast. We had a most sumptuous feast, or so it appeared to us, inured as we were to plain Camp fare. I was particularly pleased with the flavour of the honey, which Victoria informed me was taken from a hive in the garden. The milk, too, was good and plentiful, so we had at last reached the "land flowing with milk and honey."

Before we left, I asked our fair hostess how it came about that she, a Syrian damsel, was known as Victoria, to which she promptly replied, "Because I am Queen of Jericho."

Some time afterwards I made a special visit to Old Jericho. Naturally, during the 3,000 odd years that have elapsed since its capture by Joshua, the old city has got silted up and the place has been covered over by soil washed down from the Judæan hills; but just before the War a party of Antiquarians commenced excavation work and exposed several buildings of the old city, some twenty or thirty feet below the surface of the ground. There the lintels and door-posts of wood may still be seen embedded in the brickwork, but they are all turned into charcoal, probably from the fire which consumed the city by Joshua's command.

It will be remembered that the rebuilding of Jericho was forbidden under a terrible curse, "Cursed be the man before the Lord that riseth up and buildeth this city Jericho; he shall lay the foundation thereof in his firstborn, and in his youngest son shall he set up the gates of it."

The Battalion left its pleasant bivouac by the Nueiameh at 5 o'clock in the afternoon, and waded across through its cool waters; when we had marched through the appalling dust of the Valley for some three miles, I observed General Hodgson waiting to review us on the far side of a steep nullah. I cantered on, and took my place beside the General and his A.D.C., Captain Buxton.

I am certain that a review was never held under more peculiar circumstances.

The men marched in column of fours, platoon after platoon, down one side of the steep gully and up the other, and then past the General, who apparently expected to see them marching as steadily as if they had been in the Long Valley at Aldershot; and the strange part of it is that they were marching steadily, shoulder to shoulder, in spite of the difficult ground which they had to negotiate and the enormous load they had to carry. They were one mass of dust from head to foot. Nothing could be seen of their faces except a pair of eyes blinking out of a countenance which looked as if it had been dipped in a flour barrel and then streaked with lines of soot, for rivulets of black sweat ran in parallel lines down their dust-covered faces.

It was the funniest sight I ever saw in my life, but the men were as grave as owls. I could hardly keep my face straight when, on the command "eyes left" being given, they turned their comical looking faces boldly up to the General!

I remarked to him that it was a bit of an ordeal to review them just after scrambling down and up the steep sides of a gully, and he replied, "That is exactly why I am here. I want to see how they shape under the most difficult possible circumstances, and I must congratulate you on their soldierly bearing and steadiness."

The Battalion certainly did itself credit that day, for it was no light ordeal to go through, considering the dust and heat, and the enormous weight that the unfortunate men had to carry stowed away on every part of the person.

When we had completed about six miles of the march towards our camping place at the Auja, we were met by the Brigade Major of the 12th Cavalry Brigade, an energetic Staff Officer, who, besides coming himself, had thoughtfully provided guides to lead us into the

Camp in the darkness. It must be remembered that we were now within sight and range of the Turkish guns, and all large bodies of troops had to move in the dark. We were very glad to reach our bivouac on the Auja, which is a pleasant, swiftly-flowing streamlet, with many cool and shady nooks amid the foliage which grows in profusion along its banks.

CHAPTER XII

OUR POSITION IN THE MELLAHAH

We were now attached to the 12th Cavalry Brigade, commanded by Brigadier-General J. T. Wigan, and on the 16th, 17th, and 18th August we took over D and E sections of the Desert Corps front line, relieving the 19th Indian Lancers and the 6th Indian Cavalry Regiments. We were unfortunately only a few days with the 12th Brigade, which was moved to Ludd soon after we were posted to it.

The Jordan Valley, at the place where we were entrenched, is about fifteen miles wide and is over 1,200 feet below sea level. It is for the most part fairly flat, but is intersected here and there by huge ravines, which are in places quite narrow, and at others some hundreds of yards across, with sheer cliffs some thirty to fifty feet high as banks. Looking at the valley from the hills that border it, one would never suspect the existence of these great rifts. The River Jordan runs in the centre of one of these depressions, which in places is 50 to 100 feet below the ordinary level of the rest of the valley.

The Wadi Mellahah is another huge cleft or rift, running about a mile to the west of, and more or less parallel to, the Jordan. It is some 10 miles long, and varies from a few score yards to a mile in width. Steep cliffs and slopes shut it in on both sides, and make the bed of the Mellahah about as hot and stifling a spot as can well be imagined, while, to add further abomination to it, noxious fumes arose in places from its barren and desolate looking sides and bed. A tiny, briny streamlet runs its straggling course through it in the dry season, although in places it spreads out into large reed-covered

53

swamps. The water of this rivulet was so salt that a single drop was more than one could bear to take on the tip of one's tongue.

We made our headquarters in this gully some three miles from where it flows into the Auja, of which it is a tributary, and here we fixed up a reed hut as our mess house, under the shade of the only tree in this depressing spot. Of course we had to keep down in the depths of the ravine, otherwise we would be seen and shelled by the Turks.

This Mellahah Wadi had been made in the course of ages by the rush of water coming down from the Judæan range and from other hills to the north where there is a heavy annual rainfall. Here and there in the ravine, where it is at its broadest, stand isolated hillocks which the water has not worn away, and on these had been constructed some of our more northern redoubts; they were easy to defend and commanded a good view, for their tops were on a level with the surface of the surrounding valley.

One of our redoubts was named "Salt," and just to the north of it a sparkling spring bubbled out of the side of the cliff. It looked so pure and inviting that I took a mouthful, and was nearly poisoned for my pains. It was the most briny, sulphurous liquid imaginable. There is a fortune awaiting the man who exploits its medicinal properties!

The northern end of the Mellahah was held by the Turks, and there it opened out into a huge swamp. Of course the mosquitoes bred and thrived in this natural reserve, and played havoc, not only with the Turkish Army, but with our men too; when the wind blew from the north it carried the little demons amongst us in swarms. We had drained the swampy part of the Mellahah within our own lines at enormous pains, so that unless the wind blew from the north, we were fairly free of the irritating pests.

As a matter of fact we used to go out every night half a mile or so in front of our wire, deepening and diverting the streamlet, in order to dry up the swamp and remove the breeding ground of the mosquitoes as far as possible from our posts. This was always risky work, for, if the Turks had discovered what we were about, they would no doubt have made it very lively for us with rifle and machine-gun fire.

From a military point of view our position in the Mellahah was a hazardous one.

We were now on the extreme right flank and extreme north front of the British Army in Palestine—the post of honour and danger in the line, with the Turks practically on three sides of us in the salient which we held. We had the most exposed piece of front to guard which it is possible to conceive, and we were so badly supported by guns, etc., that, had the Turks made a determined attack in force, we would probably have been annihilated before succour could reach us. It was altogether an extraordinarily risky position in which to place a raw battalion. The authorities must have had great faith in our fighting abilities.

We were the only troops in the Mellahah, or within miles of it, our next nearest neighbours being the West Indian Regiment, which had a much better position than ours, close under the Judæan hills, with the swift sweet waters of the Auja running through their lines.

The 20th Indian Infantry Brigade held the Jordan some three miles to the south of us, and it would have been quite feasible for the Turks to have concentrated a considerable force and thrust themselves into the gap between our lines and theirs, and by so doing we would have been completely cut off.

The Anzac Mounted Division was strung out a long way southward, from the Auja to the Dead Sea, and some considerable time would have to elapse before these doughty warriors could come to our assistance. The guns guarding our section of the front were very few—about six 13-pounders and a couple of howitzers, the latter being rarely brought into action.

We had in our neighbourhood part of the 4th Turkish Army, some 10,000 strong, with over 70 guns, so it can be seen how precarious our position was. In our infant days some wag had bestowed upon us the unofficial motto of "No advance without security," but here we did not live up to it, for we were indeed well advanced without any security.

The Turks were in possession of the important Umm esh Shert Ford on the Jordan, and held very strong positions covering the ford on our side of the river, and their entrenched line ran right across our front and onward to the Judæan foothills, some ten miles to the west of our position.

To the southward of the Umm esh Shert Ford we had an observation post on the cliffs which overlooked the Jordan, and on a moonlight night it was an eerie experience to stroll across to it and lie on the warm sand, listening to the melancholy howling of the jackals and hyenas which filled the air with their dismal cries and wailings. I often wondered if the thick growth of tangled trees and shrubs which spread out over 100 feet below me up and down the river banks did not conceal many strange wild creatures, still unsuspected in these regions; the place lends itself to the weird in all things, but the only uncanny thing I saw there was a reddish coloured hare with enormous ears, which, on that occasion at all events, got away safely to the shelter of the reeds.

The Turkish outposts at this point were established on the

opposite bank of the Jordan, but they never molested us, or attempted to cross at this point.

Our sector of some seven miles of front stretched from this point in a north-westerly direction, and we held a series of redoubts, some on the Jordan bank of the Wadi Mellahah, others on hillocks in the ravine, as I have already described, and three more on the right bank of the Wadi.

This sector was divided into two. I placed Major Ripley in command of the north-western part, while Major Neill commanded the south-eastern wing. Each of these officers had some six redoubts to defend, and several of the posts were quite isolated and had to depend entirely on themselves in case of attack.

I recommended that two of these posts should be abolished, for they were unsuitable for defence purposes. The Corps Commander (General Chauvel), the Divisional Commander, and all their staffs came out one day to see if my suggestion was sound. I remember we all stood in a row looking over one of the parapets of the useless redoubt in full view of the Turks; if they had only fired a lucky shot from "Jericho Jane" that morning they might have made a good bag!

All the generals agreed that the two posts were useless, so we dismantled them gladly, for it meant less men to find for duty each night—a most important consideration when one's men are all too few for the work in hand.

This was the last I saw of General Chauvel and General Hodgson, for they were soon afterwards ordered out of the Valley to prepare for the great concentration which was being secretly carried out on the extreme left of the Army near Jaffa. When the Australian Division was removed we were attached to Major-General Sir Edward Chaytor, who commanded the Anzac Mounted Division of immortal fame. This was a piece of rare good fortune for us, for we found in General Chaytor a man of wide sympathy and understanding, a demon for work and efficiency, but always ready to give honour where honour was due—even unto Jews.

Although our position in the Mellahah was such an isolated and precarious one, we had no pessimistic forebodings with regard to our ability to give a good account of ourselves if attacked. We felt that "the greater the danger, the greater the honour," and it behoved us to be all the more vigilant, and up and doing at all times.

The magnificent way in which the men responded to the call of duty in that desolate, nerve-racking region, is beyond all praise. All day long the sun beat down mercilessly on them, their only shelter being a flimsy bit of bivouac canvas, and the nights were stifling. Perspiration streamed from every pore, even when resting.

Flies and mosquitoes deprived everyone of sleep, for our mosquito nets soon became torn and worthless, and could not be replaced.

Just before dark every available man other than those required to go on patrols and reconnoitring duty had to parade fully equipped and march to his post on the redoubts. Here the apparently endless night was spent. At dawn the men marched back to their comfortless bivouacs to snatch what repose they could before they were again called upon to work on strengthening the redoubts and deepening the trenches.

It was in truth an exceedingly strenuous life under such terrible climatic conditions.

Water could only be obtained in very limited quantities; every drop had to be carried from the Auja four or five miles away. The whole place was constantly enveloped in stagnant dust, so it can be imagined with what appetite a man could tackle food under such appalling conditions, every mouthful of which was necessarily full of sand and grit.

An Australian summed up life in the Jordan Valley very well, when he remarked one sweltering day, "God need not have troubled to make Hell when He had the Jordan Valley."

This part of the Jordan Valley is not supposed to be habitable during the months of August and September. Even the wild Bedouins, who linger in these parts to feed their flocks of goats, flee from the accursed place in these two dreaded months.

No British soldier had yet been called upon to endure the horrors of the Mellahah even for a week; nevertheless the Jewish Battalion was kept there for over seven weeks at the most deadly period of the year. Looking back upon it all I can only say that the Jewish people may well be proud of their Battalion for the admirable way it "carried on" in this abomination of desolation. It was about the hottest, most unhealthy, and most God-forsaken place in the universe—in fact some of my men assured me that they saw the Devil himself there, horns, tail and all!

Such was the position allotted to the 38th Battalion to defend and hold, and it can be imagined that the change from the hill tops of Ephraim to this inferno was appalling.

Knowing that our enemies had already tried to abolish the Jewish Battalion, I was strongly reminded of the story of Uriah the Hittite!

How terribly we suffered owing to our tour of duty in this pestilential region will be described in a later chapter.

57

CHAPTER XIII

LIFE IN MELLAHAH

Although the climatic change from the cool hill-tops of Samaria to the inferno of the Jordan Valley differed as does Heaven from Hell, still we had compensations in the fair, just, and kindly treatment meted out to us by General Chaytor and every officer, non-commissioned officer, and man of the Anzac Mounted Division.

The battalion stood entirely on its merits, and that it found favour in the sight of these famous fighters is the proudest feather in its cap. Their minds were as broad as the wide spaces from whence they had come, and in their strong souls there was no room for petty spite or discrimination. If we quitted ourselves like men and performed our duties like good soldiers, then it did not matter, even if we were Jews.

The Anzac Mounted Division Headquarters were about eight miles from my own, and it frequently fell to my lot to ride there through the devouring heat of the day for a conference with the General. Never shall I forget the delicious cool draught of shandy that always welcomed me, straight from the ice-box, mixed by the cunning hand of Colonel Bruxner, the A.A. and Q.M.G. of the Division. Bruxner would spy me from afar off, and, being a man of understanding, had the nectar all ready by the time I reached his tent, and oh, how good it was! No place in the world can raise a thirst like the Jordan Valley, but it was almost worth enduring when it could be quenched by a long draught of Bruxner's elixir.

The principal objective on our special piece of front was the Umm esh Shert Ford over the Jordan. It was some two miles to the East of our most northerly posts on the Mellahah, and it was well protected by a series of trenches, by barbed wire entanglements, and by the fortified Jordan cliffs. If we could, by any chance, get possession of this crossing, it would mean that the Turkish communications would be thrown considerably out of gear, and all their local arrangements East and West of the Jordan completely upset.

Furthermore, in the case of an advance on our part, by pushing mounted troops across this Ford, the whole of the Turkish position, ten miles to the East-South-East of us at Nimrin, would be turned, for the road by the Umm esh Shert Ford was the short cut to Es Salt (the old Ramoth Gilead) and Amman (the ancient Rabbath

Ammon, where that splendid Hittite soldier Uriah was treacherously sent to his death).

Our constant endeavour, therefore, in patrol and reconnaissance, was to gather all possible information as to the ways and means of getting at this spot and making it our own. No stone was left unturned and no risk avoided which would lead to this important result, and in due course we had our reward.

In such an isolated position as ours, the only thing to be done was to adopt an aggressive attitude towards our enemies and so induce them to think that we were a great deal stronger than was actually the case. This policy succeeded admirably, and we put up such a good bluff, and harried the Turks so vigorously, that they were in constant dread of attack, and immediately began to erect barbed wire fences right along their entire front, with every appearance of haste and nervousness.

Considering the nature and extent of the position which we held, we lost very few men in killed, wounded, and missing during the seven odd weeks we grilled in the Jordan Valley. We were daily and nightly shelled, but the Turkish gunners rarely had any luck. On the other hand we harassed them continuously, with the result that deserters began to come in freely, sometimes singly, and often in twos and threes. It is strange, but true, that until we came into the valley, prisoners and deserters were very scarce.

On one occasion a prisoner was brought before me trembling violently. On asking him what was the matter, he replied that he feared his throat was about to be cut! His officer, he said, had told him that we finished off all our prisoners in this way. I laughed, and (wishing to prove him) told him that after he had had some food I proposed to send him back to his camp so that he might tell all his comrades how well we treated those who fell into our hands. On hearing this he cried bitterly that he did not want to return to his camp at any price, and begged to be kept by the British, a request to which I of course readily acceded.

A Turkish sergeant who was captured one day made us all laugh heartily. Before he was marched off to the prisoners' compound somebody wanted to take a photo of him. The little sergeant (for he was quite diminutive) preened himself like a peacock, gave a rakish tilt to his headgear, a fierce twist to his moustache, and struck a dramatic pose before he would allow himself to be snapped. He was a regular Turkish Charley Chaplin!

Most of our prisoners told us quite frankly that they were tired of the war, their ill usage, and bad food, and were glad to be in our hands, more especially as they never got any rest in front of our lines.

59

On the 26th August thirteen Turks of the 1st Infantry Battalion of the 2nd Regiment of the 24th Division surrendered. These men deserted en bloc while they were holding a post which guarded the flank of their battalion. I found out from them that their relief party was due to arrive before I could possibly get a half platoon from my battalion to occupy the deserted post. If time had allowed me to lay a little trap, I should like to have seen the faces of the incoming Turks when they found themselves looking down our rifle barrels as they marched into their post. They must have been sufficiently astonished as it was to find the place empty.

I watched an exciting little adventure one morning as I stood in one of the fire bays of our most advanced redoubt, just as dawn was breaking, peering through my field glasses to the northward, along the jagged course of the Mellahah where it spread out into many channels and ravines near the Turkish lines.

All at once I spied, some 800 yards off, two Turkish officers standing at the foot of a huge sand slope, gazing at something away to their left. They looked to me as if they had come out to shoot a hare, or perhaps a gazelle, as there were some of these pretty creatures in the Valley. One of the officers was extremely tall and wore a long black cloak.

Now I knew that I had an officer (Lieutenant Evans) and man out scouting in that neighbourhood, and I felt rather anxious for their safety if they should, unexpectedly, come upon the Turks. I therefore searched the vicinity with my glasses, and sure enough, there they were walking calmly along on the opposite side of the high sand bank under which the Turks were standing. Neither party was aware of the presence of the other. I felt it was not a time to take any chances, for I did not know how many more Turks there might be concealed from my view behind the many sand hills that were dotted about, so I called up Major Ripley and sent him and half-a-dozen men at the double, to cause a diversion, and, if possible, to capture the enemy officers.

While giving these directions I kept my glasses on my two scouts, hoping that a lucky turn would take them out of danger, or expose the enemy to them before they themselves were spotted. All at once Lieutenant Evans headed up the side of the sand ridge, and I knew then that all would be well, for the Turks had their backs to him. As soon as he reached the top he cautiously peered over, and he must have been astonished to see the enemy so near, for he promptly ducked his head out of view. He then slid down the slope, took his orderly with him, and ran to put himself between the Turks and their lines, hoping, I suppose, to ambush them as they returned. The latter, all unconscious of what was going on, were taking things very casually, and instead of going back to camp, they came on a little way in the direction of our lines. This upset Evans' calculations, so he and his man began to stalk the Turks, and just as he was about to open fire on them they discovered him, and then both sides loosed off their rifles and a regular duel began.

Meanwhile Major Ripley and his men had climbed half-way up the side of the ravine, and they in turn began to blaze away at the Turks, who were now thoroughly scared. They took to flight, and in the many twists, turns and channels thereabouts managed to get safely away to their own lines.

Evans and his scout got back to ours, none the worse for their adventure.

I had a narrow shave myself in this same post a couple of days later. It was my custom to scan the enemy's lines soon after daybreak every morning from this commanding position in order to see if any changes had taken place in the night. A Turkish sniper must have seen me and marked me for his own. At all events I had just finished my survey, and stepped down from my perch, when a bullet buried itself with a thud in the bank just where my head had been!

A couple of days later Lieutenant Mendes and Sergeant Levy were out scouting along the intricate course of the Mellahah, to the north of our lines, when they walked into an ambuscade; the Sergeant fell at the first volley, but luckily Mendes was not hit. He refused to surrender, and, in spite of some fleet-footed Turks making the pace very hot for him, he eluded the lot and got back to our lines safely, but thoroughly exhausted.

CHAPTER XIV

WE WIN OUR FIRST HONOURS

On the 28th August a patrol of six privates, under the command of a sergeant, crept up to the Turkish trenches near the Umm esh Shert Ford. It was a dark and windy night, so they got quite close to the enemy without being seen. When about thirty yards short of the Turks they lay down and then observed a sentry standing a little way off. One of the patrol, Private Sapieshvili, a Jew from the Caucasus, began to crawl forward and cautiously stalk the unwary sentinel. When eventually he succeeded in getting behind him, he stood up and advanced boldly, pretending to be a Turk, for he was able to speak a few words of Turkish. All at once he pounced on the sentry, seized him by the throat and bore him to the ground.

The enemy in the trenches heard the scuffle and opened fire and one man of our patrol was badly hit. Sapieshvili, however, stuck to his prisoner, disarmed him and took him triumphantly off to our camp. The Turks in the trenches numbered about a score, and kept up a heavy fire, so the rest of the patrol withdrew. Before doing so, Private Gordon lifted his wounded comrade (Private Marks) and carried him back to our lines under a rain of bullets from the Turks.

I recommended these men to General Chaytor for their gallantry and coolness under fire.

It was unfortunate that Private Marks' wound proved to be a mortal one. He had only joined the battalion some three days previously, and this was his first encounter with the Turks. He had served in France and other war centres, and had passed through many a fierce fight scathless.

We gave him a very impressive burial the following morning, under the lea of a little hillock, with his face turned towards Jerusalem; the spires of the buildings on the Mount of Olives could actually be seen from the spot where we were standing around his grave.

One of the ten men who, at Helmieh, had wished to join a Labour battalion, but who, on reconsideration, had seen that it was his duty to remain as a fighting soldier, was Private Greyman. He was a man who disapproved of all forms of violence. He hated war and all the brutalities pertaining thereto, yet he carried out his military duties most conscientiously. He happened to be one of a party on duty in the forward trenches on the Day of Atonement, and while repelling some snipers who were attempting to make it unpleasant for us in our camp, poor Greyman met with an instantaneous death, an enemy bullet passing through his head. I heard afterwards that when his widow received the usual War Office notification that he was killed in action, she refused to believe it, for she saw that the date given was the Day of Atonement, a day on which she said no Jew could possibly be fighting; but alas, we had to man the trenches continuously, no matter how sacred or in what reverence any particular day was held by Jew or Gentile.

We were sometimes attached to the 1st and sometimes to the 2nd Australian Light Horse Brigades under Generals Cox and Ryrie; when they moved we were placed under General Meldrum, the

Commander of the New Zealand Mounted Rifles Brigade. All were keen soldiers and good and gallant comrades.

While we were under General Ryrie I remember he said to me one day that he would like to come out and inspect my posts.

"Very good, General," I said. "Come out with me any morning you wish."

"When do you start?" he asked.

"Generally at 3 a.m.," I replied.

"That's a d—d good time to sleep," said the General.

Another night some of our patrols scared the Turks badly, and they started a tremendous fusillade with every rifle and gun that could be brought into action. The noise of the battle reverberated down the Mellahah and reached the Auja, where General Ryrie was encamped. Thinking that a serious attack had begun, the General sprang hastily out of bed and planted his naked foot right on to the tail of a huge black scorpion. For a full half-hour afterwards Australia was heard at her best.

When I saw him a couple of days later he philosophically remarked that there was virtue even in a scorpion sting, for it had completely cured him of ever attempting to get out of bed again in the dark, even if all the Turks in the Ottoman Empire were at his door.

General Ryrie, afterwards promoted to Major-General, was appointed to the command of the Australian Mounted Division, and had the K.C.M.G. conferred on him.

Towards the end of August General Allenby reviewed the Anzacs at their Headquarters, some four miles to the north of Jericho. The Mounted Division was formed into three sides of a square, and into this General Allenby galloped, followed by his Staff. It was well for the Commander-in-Chief that he was a good horseman, for the spirited animal which he rode gave one or two very hearty bucks, quite enough to have unseated the majority of our Generals.

Later, the Chief decorated a number of the officers and men who had gallantly won distinctions, and at the end of the ceremony made a good soldierly speech to the Division.

I was invited to be present at the review, and on being presented by General Chaytor to the Commander-in-Chief the latter remarked, "Oh, by the way, Patterson, I fear I cannot form your Jewish Brigade, for I have been notified by the War Office that there are no more Jewish troops coming out." I replied that I thought this information must be inaccurate, for I had just had a letter from the officer commanding the 40th Battalion at Plymouth, informing me that he was about to embark with his battalion for service in

Palestine. The Commander-in-Chief seemed somewhat surprised on hearing this, but remarked that he considered his information later and better than mine, so of course there was nothing more to be said.

A few days afterwards, on 30th August, General Chaytor had a conference with all his Brigade and Infantry Commanders, and as he had heard General Allenby saying to me that he considered his information with regard to Jewish reinforcements better than mine, he remarked: "Well, Patterson, your information about the coming of the other Jewish Battalions was better than the Chief's after all, for one of my officers has just come from England, and he tells me that a strong Jewish Battalion came out with him in the same ship and landed in Egypt a couple of days ago."

As I considered it only right to let the Commander-in-Chief know that the information he had received was not accurate, I wrote and told him that I understood that another Jewish Battalion, some 1,400 strong, had already arrived in Egypt.

In reply to this I got a memorandum from the Chief of Staff, Major-General Louis Jean Bols, intimating that in future I was only to address the Commander-in-Chief through the ordinary channels of communication.

It was evident from this that the Chief of Staff was not pleased that the Commander-in-Chief should have any sidelight from me on Jewish affairs. Of course this had long been apparent, for anything I had previously written through the ordinary channels—no matter how important to the welfare of the battalion—had invariably been returned to me with the remark that it was not considered necessary to refer the matter further.

Some months after my interview with the Commander-in-Chief yet another thousand men arrived from England, and altogether there were over five thousand Jewish soldiers serving in the Jewish units in Palestine. The formation of a Jewish Brigade had been the definite policy of the War Office, and an intimation to this effect had been sent to General Allenby. The Commander-in-Chief of the E.E.F. had himself written to me to say that a Jewish Brigade would be formed, yet this promise, which meant so much to the comfort and efficiency of the men and to the prestige of Jews the world over, was never fulfilled; instead, we were pushed about from Brigade to Brigade and from Division to Division in the most heart-breaking manner, with the result that we got all the kicks and none of the traditional halfpence!

In the space of three months we were shunted about like so many cattle trucks and found ourselves, in that brief period, attached to no less than twelve different formations of the British Army!

General Chaytor gave a great lift to the spirit of the battalion when he conferred the Military Medal on Privates Sapieshvili and Gordon for their gallant conduct on the night patrol already mentioned. We had a special parade in "Salt" post redoubt, after Divine Service on the first day of the Jewish New Year (7th September, 1918). Before all their comrades the General recounted their gallant deeds, pinned the coveted ribbons on their breasts, and then ordered the battalion to march past and salute—not himself, but the two men whom he had just decorated. From this moment General Chaytor had with him the heartfelt devotion of every man in the unit. A small thing can win the respect, goodwill, and devotion of a Regiment, but it is not every General who has the knack of gaining it.

CHAPTER XV

CAPTURE OF THE UMM ESH SHERT FORD

As the date fixed for the great advance of the Army in Palestine drew near, certain parts of the Jordan Valley began to look very comical. Here and there would be seen a battery of artillery parked, or a cavalry regiment, with its horses tethered in neat and orderly array, in the most approved army style, but on closer inspection both horses and guns were found to be merely dummies! Great camps were pitched, but there was not a soldier in them; fires were lighted all over the place at dusk, as if a mighty army were bivouacked round about, and every conceivable kind of bluff was put up in order to deceive the Turks and make them think that the long expected attack was to be made through Gilead, to effect a junction with the Arab Army of the Hedjaz. The Jewish Battalion was even ordered to march and counter march from Jericho to the Dead Sea by some wight at G.H.Q. who still remembered us, but General Chaytor scotched this stunt, for of course he knew it was quite impossible for us to guard our front throughout the night and march some forty miles by day as well in that terrific heat.

There were really very few troops in the Valley, if one considers the enemy force that could have been concentrated against us. According to General Allenby's despatch, there were some 6,000 rifles, 2,000 sabres, and 74 guns facing us in the Jordan Valley.

General Allenby in his despatch of the 31st October, 1918, writes:—

"By reducing the strength of the troops in the Jordan Valley to a minimum," etc., and "To prevent the decrease in strength in the Jordan Valley being discovered by the enemy I ordered Major General Sir Edward Chaytor, K.C.M.G., C.B., A.D.C., to carry out with the Australian and New Zealand Mounted Division, the 20th Indian (Imperial Service) Infantry Brigade, the 38th and 39th Battalions of the Royal Fusiliers, and the 1st and 2nd Battalions British West Indies Regiment a series of demonstrations with the object of inducing the enemy to believe that an attack East of the Jordan was intended, either in the direction of Madeba or Amman.

"The enemy was thought to be anticipating an attack in these directions and every possible step was taken to strengthen his suspicions."

On the 15th September the 39th Battalion Royal Fusiliers, under the command of Colonel Margolin, D.S.O., arrived in the Jordan Valley, and took up its position on the Auja in support of the 38th Battalion in the line.

A couple of days before the big offensive which began on the 18th September, General Allenby visited my Headquarters, where I presented to him all the officers not on duty. He took me a little apart and asked me if I was sure I could trust the men to fight, and I assured him that he need have no anxiety on that score, for the men were all right and would respond to any call when it was made.

He then asked me if there was any other point I should like to bring to his notice: I told him that malaria was daily becoming more prevalent and I was losing 200 men a week from this cause alone: I also pointed out that I did not think that the medical arrangements for the evacuation and care of the men were all that they should be. The General made a note of this in his book.

The only result was that I got an irate letter from the Deputy Adjutant-General asking me for a full report as to why I had misinformed the Commander-in-Chief about my sick, and about medical matters generally, so that on the morning of the 23rd September, the day we were ordered to pursue the enemy, when I

66

should have been solely devoted to the leading of my men and all the problems pertaining thereto, I had to sit down and smooth the ruffled feathers of the Deputy Adjutant-General.

I not only proved my case to the hilt, but emphasized it by giving further evidence which I had not troubled the Commander-in-Chief by recounting.

General Chaytor specially warned us that, during the offensive on our left, we were to increase our patrols and harry the enemy as much as possible, to keep him in his lines and to prevent, if possible, any large force of Turks crossing from the East of the Jordan to reinforce their armies holding the line from the Jordan to the sea.

This is how the official report runs:—"Chaytor's force in the Jordan Valley had so far confined itself to vigorous patrolling to insure that the enemy could make no move without their knowledge. The rôle of this composite force was to secure the right flank of the army and the Jordan crossings, to keep in close touch with the enemy and take advantage of any withdrawal on their part, but to run no risk of being involved with a more powerful foe too early in the battle. This difficult task was admirably carried out."

During the nights of the 18th, 19th, 20th and 21st September we made demonstrations against the Turkish positions along our front. Parties would crawl out into favourable positions, such as a fold in the ground, and open fire all down the line. This always made the Turks nervy, and their trenches would be manned and every individual would blaze away for all he was worth.

On the 19th and 20th they got so "windy" that they called on their artillery to put down a barrage to prevent us from making an assault. Each time the barrage was put down our men were well clear, and lay snug and safe until the enemy had uselessly expended hundreds of rounds, when they quietly returned to camp, not a whit the worse for all the cannonading. There was very little sleep on these nights for anyone, and the Jewish Battalion certainly did all that in it lay to further the intentions of the Commander-in-Chief by holding every Turk in the neighbourhood of the Jordan closely to his lines.

On the 20th we pushed well up against the Turkish trenches, found them all manned, and again drew heavy rifle, machine-gun and artillery fire. We had a few men wounded in this affair. Why we had not a heavy casualty list on these occasions is a mystery to me, for the men had to advance in the open over a stretch of ground as level as a billiard table.

Number 6 Trench Mortar Battery R.A. was under my command in the Mellahah, and I ordered this battery to open fire on the Turkish position round Umm esh Shert, if we should find difficulty in ousting the enemy from this important place.

I had arranged to attack this position on the 22nd September, but at midnight on the 21st my Intelligence Officer sent me news that the enemy's resistance in the trenches opposite Umm esh Shert Ford was weakening.

I immediately ordered out my reserve, and sent them under Lieutenant Cross to reinforce Major Neill, whose duty it was to push in the Turks and take the Ford at the earliest possible moment. I got favourable news by telephone of the steady advance of the men; trench after trench was occupied, and when I left my Headquarters at 4 a.m. for the scene of the fight, I was able to report to General Chaytor's Staff Officer that we were almost in possession of the crossing.

I galloped off as dawn was breaking, scrambled up the cliffs and across the ground from which the Turks had fled, and arrived in time to go down with Major Neill, Captain Julian, and Lieutenants Jabotinsky and Cross, to take possession of this coveted passage over the Jordan. I may mention here that Jabotinsky had been attached to G.H.Q. for special work, but, as soon as the battalion went into the line, he requested to be returned to duty in order to share in all our dangers and hardships.

The moment we had secured the Umm esh Shert Ford I signalled the news to General Chaytor, who immediately took advantage of our capture by pushing mounted troops across the Jordan, thus outflanking the Turks who held the foothills of Shunat Nimrin, which barred the way to Es Salt.

The 1st Australian Light Horse Brigade crossed while we covered the Ford with our rifles and machine-guns, and they never drew rein until Es Salt was reached that evening, where a large force of the enemy with guns, etc., was captured by the Anzac Mounted Division.

That same afternoon, two companies of the 39th Battalion Royal Fusiliers moved up to our support and took up position in the posts which we had vacated in the Mellahah.

It is a curious fact that the whole movement of the British Army in Palestine, which swept the Turks out of the country, was actually pivoted on the sons of Israel, who were once again fighting the enemy, not far from the spot where their forefathers had crossed the Jordan under Joshua.

CHAPTER XVI

THE LOST TRANSPORT WAGONS

Meanwhile I was ordered to clear away the enemy believed to be still holding the ground to the north of our trenches round Red Hill. I detailed Captain H. H. Harris and his Company for this duty, the remainder of the battalion taking up position in the vacated Turkish trenches overlooking the Jordan. Lieutenant Jabotinsky, with his platoon, took possession of Umm esh Shert and put the captured ford in a state of defence, making machine-gun emplacements, etc., to cover the crossing.

I myself with Captain Julian, Lieutenant Cross, and a platoon reconnoitred up the river, for I had heard that there was a bridge in existence, which had been thrown across by the Turks in the neighbourhood of the ford, and I was anxious to find it if possible. After going some little way I found it was nearly 8 o'clock a.m., and time to be getting back to my Battalion Headquarters, so I left Julian, Cross, and the patrol to push on and make what discoveries they could along the river. When I got back to my tent I found a telegram awaiting me from General Chaytor which informed me that I had been given command of a body of troops to be known officially as "Patterson's Column." It was composed of the 38th and 39th Battalions Royal Fusiliers, and was ordered to concentrate on the Auja bridgehead.

I handed over command of the 38th to Major Ripley, who was the next Senior Officer, and issued the necessary concentration orders.

Later on I rode out to view the position which we had wrested from the Turks on the Jordan and, on the way, I was surprised to meet Captain Julian being brought in wounded on a camel. He was in considerable pain, but quite cheery and able to give me a full account of what had happened. It seems that soon after I had left them the party was ambushed by the Turks, who caught them, in the neighbourhood of Red Hill, with machine-gun and rifle fire. Julian, Cross, and Private Mildemer fell; the remainder of the patrol melted into a fold of the ground and made their escape. Julian, although severely wounded in the foot, also managed to get away, aided by Corporal Elfman, who gallantly helped him to safety, although under heavy fire from the enemy.

Reinforcements had been sent out as quickly as possible to the scene of the fight by the nearest Company, but by the time they arrived the Turks had gone. No trace could be found of Lieutenant Cross's body, but Private Mildemer was found lying dead where he fell.

On receipt of this news I sent another party under Lieutenant Bullock to give burial according to Jewish rites to the gallant man who had fallen, and to make a thorough search of the locality for Lieutenant Cross's body, but no trace of the missing officer could be found. Telegrams were dispatched to the hospitals at Amman, Deraa, and to Damascus after we had captured that city, but nothing was known of him at any of these places, and in the end we all came to the sad conclusion that we had seen the last of poor Cross and that the Turks must have thrown his body into the Jordan after he had died from his wounds. His loss cast a gloom over the battalion.

I was also exceedingly sorry to be deprived of Captain Julian's services with the transport, just at the moment when we were ordered to start off in pursuit of the enemy, for he was an ideal Transport Officer, and never once let the battalion down while he served in that capacity, and he had held this important position from the day he joined us.

It was not long until we had a sharp reminder of his loss, for that same evening our transport trekked off and could not be found anywhere. Someone (I never could discover who) gave the Transport Sergeant orders to leave his lines on the Auja and report, with all wagons, etc., to Major Ripley in the Mellahah. In the darkness he failed to find the Major, and on the morning of the 23rd not a single soul in the battalion knew anything about where the Transport had gone, or how it could be found. They had completely vanished from the ken of everybody, taking with them our food, forage, cooking pots, and spare ammunition. The new Transport Officer, Captain Cunningham, who had been detailed to take Captain Julian's place, was unable to find any trace of them when he went to take over charge. They had mysteriously disappeared from their bivouac and gone off into the blue.

This was a very disturbing factor in the situation, for we had orders to start off in pursuit of the enemy at 2 o'clock a.m. next morning. Cunningham, Quartermaster Smythe, and all available men who could be pressed into the service, were sent in every direction to run the Transport to earth.

Eventually Smythe came back to say that he had been tracking wagon wheels for at least five miles, but they could not be ours, for the tracks led steadily in a northerly direction towards the Turkish lines.

After duly strafing Major Ripley for having, this early in his command, lost his transport, I set off in quest of the rovers.

Luckily my charger Betty was in splendid condition, and I certainly put her on her mettle that morning. I took up the trail that Smythe had abandoned, followed it for seven or eight miles at a steady canter, and then lost all trace on hard ground. I had to cast round in a big circle before I found it once more, then I went on again for another three or four miles when I met some Australians. On asking them if they had seen a column of wagons going northward they said, "No, we have been along here for a couple of miles, but we have seen nothing."

This was very disheartening news, and I almost felt inclined to give up the quest in this direction and turn back; but having come so far, I made up my mind to go on, even to the Turkish lines themselves, before I gave up the hunt.

I was then about eight miles short of the Turkish position, or what had been the Turkish position at the foot of the hills towards which the tracks still led.

When I had covered another few miles, to my inexpressible relief, I at last caught sight of the Transport, steadily pursuing its way northward!

I made Betty put on an extra spurt and soon caught them up. It is lucky that there was no grass about, or the prairie itself would have caught fire when I at last overtook the Transport Sergeant. The language addressed to the jackdaw by the Cardinal Lord Archbishop of Rheims was angel talk compared to mine.

When I ordered him sharply to get back at once to where he came from, he was so confused that he promptly turned his horse round and began to ride off towards camp—leaving his baggage wagons still calmly proceeding in the opposite direction.

I called the dazed sergeant back and told him very forcibly to halt the column and take the wagons back as quickly as possible to his original camp. I was never able to get any satisfactory information from the sergeant (who by the way was a Welshman and a Christian) as to what induced him to trek off into the unknown in such a mad fashion. I can only imagine that the devil, who lives in the Jordan Valley, had impersonated Major Ripley and had ordered the sergeant to push for all he was worth for the Turkish lines, leaving us without food, water, cooking pots, or ammunition—in fact leaving us "beggars by the wayside."

My chase of the transport wasted some precious hours, but I was back in camp soon after 10 a.m., where I found the battalion full of bustle and activity, preparing for concentration on the Auja bridgehead.

71

On my return to Headquarters I found that Major Ripley was ill and only fit for hospital. He had had a most nerve-shattering time while commanding his section; for his posts were very much exposed and there was always the dread and anxiety of an attack in overwhelming numbers. Sleep rarely comes to soothe a man's nerves in such trying circumstances, especially in the awful heat we endured in the Mellahah; in fact, Major Ripley's features had wasted away so much owing to the worry and anxiety of all he had undergone that he reminded me of nothing so much as one of the mummified birds I had once seen in a cave of Upper Egypt. I never saw Major Ripley again in the battalion, but I am glad to say he made an excellent recovery, and was eventually given a good staff job in Alexandria.

I gave the command of the battalion to Major Neill, and from that moment I had no further anxieties, outside my own province, with which to contend.

CHAPTER XVII

WE GO UP TO RAMOTH GILEAD

When I took command of the Column I chose Captain Douglas Leadley as my Staff Officer, and a better man it would be almost impossible to find. I never knew Leadley to forget anything, and it was a great relief to feel that when once I had given him any instructions, I need have no further anxiety about them, for he was absolutely reliable and competent in every way.

When Leadley came to me, Major Neill selected Captain T. B. Brown to replace him as Adjutant of the 38th Battalion, and an excellent staff officer he made, as far as I could judge.

The concentration on the Auja bridgehead proceeded as rapidly as possible, for the Column had to move soon after midnight.

I found that the 38th Battalion could not possibly concentrate in time, for Captain H.H. Harris's Company was many miles to the north, where it had been sent in pursuit of the enemy. I therefore ordered Major Neill to follow me as quickly as possible to Shunat

Nimrin, a position on the Moab foothills, some ten miles to the eastward of the Auja.

At 2 a.m. on the 24th, Column Headquarters and the 39th Battalion crossed the Jordan at the Auja bridgehead, scrambled up the steep Jordan cliffs, and marched on towards Nimrin.

General Chaytor had meanwhile ordered an advance upon Es Salt (the ancient Ramoth Gilead) and Amman, with his whole force, which consisted of the Anzac Mounted Division (less one squadron), a field battery, a heavy battery, two mountain batteries, Patterson's Column, the 20th Indian Infantry Brigade, and the 1st and 2nd Battalions British West Indies Regiment.

The mounted troops pushed forward rapidly, and soon out-distanced the infantry and guns. The Anzacs were such gluttons for battle that they broke down every resistance and completely destroyed and broke up the enemy before the Infantry could come into action.

The 20th Indian Infantry and the guns followed the horsemen, for, from their position on the Jericho-Es Salt road, they were much better situated to take the lead than any other dismounted troops.

My Column struck the advancing troops at Nimrin, where I was just in time to see General Chaytor fly past in a motor car. The General always believed in being well to the front when there was a fight on, and has been known on more than one occasion to be mixed up in the fray itself.

My orders were to form the rearguard to Chaytor's Force, and all day long the main Column wound its way slowly past Nimrin until 3 o'clock in the afternoon of the 24th. I then gave the order for the 39th to advance, and left orders for the 38th, on arrival at Nimrin, to follow on to Es Salt.

It was interesting to observe the strong positions from which we had driven the Turks, and to see overturned cannon, limbers, wagons, ammunition carts strewing the road; "Jericho Jane," an enormous gun that used to fire into Jericho, the Divisional Headquarters, and generally rake us all round, was lying ignominiously on her back in a ditch; dead bodies of men, horses, and draught bullocks made the world unpleasant in their vicinity; Bedouins flocked around like locusts, looting machine guns, rifles, ammunition and stores of all kinds which had been abandoned by the Turks in their hasty flight. The Arabs in these parts had the time of their lives, for loot is to them as honey to the bee.

General Chaytor had left word at Nimrin that he wished to see me, so I was anxious to get on to Es Salt as quickly as possible, where I hoped to find him. I therefore gave all necessary

73

instructions to Colonel Margolin, and, leaving Captain Leadley with him in case anything unforeseen should crop up, and he should require the assistance of my Staff Officer, I rode on as fast as possible to Es Salt, taking my groom with me.

After great difficulty and much squeezing we forced our way through the miles and miles of wagons, baggage, guns, etc., which were slowly and painfully crawling up the steep mountain side towards Es Salt. I arrived there at about 9 p.m., but failed to find the General, who had already pushed further ahead. I was hospitably entertained by the Indian Infantry Brigade, and4 afterwards turned aside, and, tethering my horse, lay down a little way off the road, with my saddle for my pillow, glad to have a blanket to wrap round me on these heights, which felt decidedly chilly after the suffocating heat of the Mellahah. I woke up in the middle of the night just in time to recover Betty, who had broken loose and was straying off towards a forage cart. Having tied her up, I settled down again and slept until dawn. I wondered during the night how it was that my bed was so warm, and as soon as daylight came I discovered the reason—I had been sleeping on a bed of dry stable litter!

After an early cup of tea with the Indians, I pushed on through Es Salt to General Chaytor's Headquarters, which were just beyond. Here I found that the General had gone on to direct the operations which were then in progress round Amman. Major Anderson of his Staff provided me with an excellent breakfast, and soon afterwards we were joined by my friend, Colonel Bruxner, who had had a strenuous night marshalling the guns and transport on their toilsome journey up from the Valley.

I received telegraphic instruction from General Chaytor to make Es Salt my Headquarters and put it into a state of all-round defence.

I put up my "bivvy" a little way out of the town, under an enormous fig tree then laden with delicious fruit, close to the Nimrin, which flowed swiftly by, almost at the edge of our bivouac.

Colonel Margolin and the 39th took over Es Salt and at once occupied the commanding hills round about, where he was soon entrenched and ready to give the enemy a very warm reception in case of attack.

The Turks had left a number of sick and wounded soldiers at this place in a dreadful state. Captain Redcliffe Salaman took these poor wretches in hand and soon brought about a wonderful improvement in their condition. The town itself was in a state of indescribable filth, and had it not been for the unceasing efforts of Captain Salaman and the Sanitary Department which he organised, an outbreak of typhoid or other dreadful disease must have ensued.

No praise is too high for the work which Salaman did during the period he was in Medical charge at Es Salt.

Soon after we had established ourselves here I found that the Bedouins were looting the abandoned Turkish munitions, stores, etc., right and left; as they were our allies, I did not want to interfere without orders, so I reported the matter to General Chaytor.

The General promptly wired me to stop all looting by these marauders—a proceeding which annoyed them intensely. I had to send out strong parties from the 39th Battalion to patrol that part of the country towards Amman, and the whole of the road from Es Salt back to Nimrin had, in addition, to be watched and guarded. The 39th patrolled the country from Es Salt as far as the El Howeij Bridge, some six miles south of Es Salt, while the 38th took up guard duty from this point to Nimrin. This was rather hard luck on the 38th, for they had almost reached Es Salt when the order to counter-march came. They had to turn and go back all that long weary way, practically without rest or food.

It was a march and counter-march that would have reflected credit on the best marching Regiment in the British Army, and no better testimonial could be given than that of Lieut. Cameron, a regular Highlander of the old school, who freely admitted that this was the very worst he had ever experienced in all his eighteen years of soldiering.

Cameron won the Military Cross, and also a bar thereto, while serving with the 38th Battalion.

Major Neill afterwards told me that he received the greatest assistance in getting the men along on this trying march from Captain H.H. Harris, who had the arduous task of shepherding the weary ones along with the rearguard.

No doubt if was one of these laggards who, some weeks afterwards, wrote me a letter full of reproaches, which made me laugh heartily, and helped to brighten the gloomy days through which I was then passing. I give an extract from a very lengthy episode:—

"You kept us in torture for six and a half weeks at Nablus. Then we left Nablus and thought after this torture you will send us for a rest, but no, you make us march to the Jordan in full marching order. You also gave us a bomb each man to put in our pocket so as to lighten the burden of the transport. You had consideration for horses, but not for humans. We travelled like pedlars to the Jordan, living on fresh air. When we reached the Jordan, it was a grand place, was it not? It surprises me you could not pick out a worse place to 4send us. Is there any worse place

than the Mellalah in this God-forsaken country? (Evidently a non-Zionist, this fellow!) You kept us in this hot hole for another six-and-a-half weeks, no other troops ever being known to stay there for more than two or three weeks—but of course anywhere was good enough for the Jews."

From the above it will be seen that at least some of the men were of the opinion that I was responsible for their troubles, while all the time I was getting into the bad books of authority in my endeavours to get them better treatment.

CHAPTER XVIII

THE CROWN OF VICTORY

The moment things were satisfactorily settled in the neighbourhood of Es Salt I hurried on to Amman. Jumping into a passing motor, I discovered that the name of the officer in the car was Lowe, and on asking him whether he was, by chance, any relation of a man I knew named Harry Lowe, he replied, "I am his brother."

On our arrival at Amman I found that General Chaytor's camp was some distance beyond the town and close to the Hedjaz Railway Station. Seeing the divisional flag flying over his tent, I made for it, and was delighted at last to run him to earth.

I heartily congratulated him on the great victory he had won in such record time. In four days his troops had covered over 60 miles; he had forced his way through the hills and mountains of Moab, a most difficult country, in the face of a superior force; he had captured the two ancient cities of Es Salt and Amman, got astride of the Hedjaz Railway, and had completely routed the 4th Turkish Army. He had captured altogether some 11,000 prisoners, some 60 guns, about 150 machine-guns, hundreds of tons of ammunition of all kinds, millions of rounds of small arms ammunition, large quantities of railway rolling-stock, and all kinds of other material, foodstuffs, horses, mules, transport wagons, motor lorries, etc.—altogether as brilliant a piece of work as was done in this or any other theatre of the Great War.

I would have those who pin their faith to the sword make a special note of the fact that not a single sabre or lance was carried by the mounted men. The hefty Anzac was able to do all that was wanted by the combination of man, horse, and rifle.

Of course Chaytor's Force lacked one great weapon, and that was a war correspondent to write up its deeds!

While I was in General Chaytor's camp a sad accident happened. A Signalling Sergeant quite close to us was examining a "dud" aerial bomb when it exploded in his hands, killing him and wounding several others.

I found Amman (the Philadelphia of the Romans) rich in old Græco-Roman architectural remains. A mighty amphitheatre, still in a fairly good state of preservation, stands out boldly amidst the ruins. Judging by the number of shattered columns and broken arches strewn about over a wide area, it must have been a very important city in the days when Rome was mistress of the world. Little or nothing of the old Rabbah Ammon is left. The walls of a very ancient citadel still crown a hill-top close by the Roman city, but whether it is the citadel which so long resisted Joab, or a later structure, I cannot say.

I remained at Amman all night, in the shadow of the great ruined amphitheatre. Once it must have rocked4 to the roar of the multitude encircling its spacious arena. Now all was silent. Only bats and owls circled through its broken arches or flew from its tilted columns, alarmed perchance by the curse of an Australian trooper sleeping uneasily amidst its ruins. While the bivouac fires yet flickered on this hoary pile I sought the shelter of a motor lorry, in which, rolled in a blanket, I lay snug and warm throughout the night.

From my own observation I can testify that the words of the Prophet Ezekiel were literally fulfilled when he wrote: "And I will make Rabbah (Ammon) a stable for camels, and the Ammonites a couching place for flocks."—(Ezekiel, Chap. XXV. verse 5.)

It must have been a very pleasant city in the old days, and I see no reason why its glories should not be revived under a stable form of Government. The country all round is fruitful and its waters sweet and abundant.

In the present straggling town there is a large colony of Circassians, and in the two previous raids made by the British on this place these people had in each case made a treacherous attack on our rearguard. The New Zealand Mounted Rifles suffered somewhat severely in the raid made on March 30th, 1918.

77

I left the ancient capital of the Ammonites soon after daybreak and, as I journeyed towards Es Salt, I had a magnificent view of the snow-capped Lebanons away in the far distance, while Gilead and Bashan lay spread out before me to the foot of Mount Hermon.

Es Salt and the hills surrounding it form the gateway to a vast rich hinterland. I have never seen grapes as large as those that grow in Gilead, or tasted any to compare with them in flavour. Figs, too, were delicious and abundant in and about Es Salt.

Rumours now began to get about that the Turkish force, still on the Hedjaz Railway to the south of Amman, would attempt to break through and try to escape northwards to Damascus by way of Nimrin.

General Chaytor ordered me to take steps to meet such an emergency, so I wired to Major Neill to put the place in a state of defence, and on September 28th I proceeded there myself and resumed command of the battalion.

While Chaytor's Force was holding the enemy on the Jordan and, later, chasing him through the Moab hills, the C.-in-C. was using the bulk of his forces in destroying the enemy holding the country to the West of the Jordan, and a very brief account of the operations may prove interesting to the reader.

In the neighbourhood of Jaffa a Franco-British force was assembled consisting of five Divisions of Infantry, a French detachment about 4,000 strong, the 5th Australian Light Horse Brigade, two brigades of mountain artillery, and eighteen batteries of heavy and siege artillery.

Carefully concealed in the orange and olive groves round about Jaffa and Ludd lay the 4th and 5th Cavalry Divisions, the Australian Mounted Division (less one Brigade), and four squadrons of French Colonial Cavalry (Spahis and Chasseurs d'Afrique).

All these were ready to dash north the moment the infantry and artillery had broken a gap in the enemy's line to the North of Jaffa.

With this highly mobile force a brilliant victory was achieved, but of course the historian will not give to the E.E.F. campaign the extravagant praise which has been lavished upon it by an ill-informed public, ignorant as yet of the fact that in the field of operations the strength of the British to that of the Turk was as that of a tiger to a tom-cat.

The bulk of the Turkish forces were on or south of a line drawn from Jisr ed Damie, on the Jordan, through Nablus and Tul Keram to the Mediterranean. His fighting strength on this front was, roughly, 17,000 Infantry, 1,000 Cavalry, and 266 guns. His line

78

of communication was long and bad. He was about 1,200 miles from his base at Constantinople, and, owing to incomplete tunnels at Amanus and Taurus and a change of gauge at Ryak, there were no less than three bad breaks in the single line of railway which had to carry his reinforcements, munitions, equipment, and food both to the Palestinian and Mesopotamian fronts.

His troops were badly fed and badly led; medical arrangements were very poor; there was considerable friction between the Turks and Germans, and the Turkish Army was composed of a mixture of races, many of them hating their masters with a fierce hatred.

Here were all the elements of a débâcle on a grand scale.

On the morning of September 19th one of the most triumphant cavalry marches ever recorded in the world's history began at Jaffa, and before the troops engaged in it drew rein in far-off Aleppo, five weeks later, they had covered some 500 miles through an enemy's country,4 captured or destroyed over 50,000 Turks, seized Damascus, Beyrout, and Aleppo, and brought to an inglorious end the Ottoman Empire.

This was no mean record for a mere handful of mounted men to accomplish. We must not forget, however, that without the lavish help of the other arms—infantry, artillery, and especially the Air Force, victory on such a colossal scale could not have been achieved.

It almost seems as if this crowning victory had been pre-ordained to take place in the year 1918. Everybody knows that the Jewish era differs from the Christian era, but perhaps not so many are aware that the Jewish year 5679 corresponds to the year 1918 of our era. A peculiarity of the Hebrew language is that every numeral has a special meaning other than that connected with time or figures. In the dim and distant past, when seers, sages, and scribes were devoutly engaged in evolving such things, was it even then pre-ordained that this crowning victory—this victory which will surely hasten the restoration of Israel—should take place in the year 5679? However that may be, it is certainly extraordinary that the figures 5, 6, 7, 9, being interpreted, should mean Ha-atereth—"Crown of Victory."

CHAPTER XIX

THE STRATEGICAL VALUE OF PALESTINE

When Turkey, unfortunately for herself, ranged her forces on the side of our enemies in the Great War she severed a friendship which had lasted for the greater part of a century. Our policy had for many years been to uphold the integrity of the Ottoman Empire because, with that Power holding Palestine, our Egyptian interests were quite safe. Now that the Turkish Empire has practically ceased to exist, Palestine becomes of cardinal importance to our Eastern interests.

Situated as it is at the Gate of the three Continents of Europe, Asia, and Africa, its strategical, political, and economic importance is beyond computation and out of all proportion to the size of this diminutive country.

Students of strategy and military history will agree that Palestine, although some distance from the Suez Canal region, dominates that main artery of our trade and commerce.

The eastern boundary of Egypt, running from Rafa on the Mediterranean to Akaba on the Gulf of that name in the Red Sea, is, from a military point of view, worthless. History tells us that all down the ages armies have crossed the Sinai Desert and worked their will on the dwellers by the Nile. Early in the War we ourselves were unable to hold this Egyptian Frontier and were forced to retire to the line of the Suez Canal. It is true we defeated the Turks there and drove them out of Egypt, but the risk to our communications was very grave. It is a risk that should never again be taken, and for the future the Suez Canal must be defended, at all events on the Eastern side, from its strategical frontier—Palestine. With a friendly people established in the Judæan strongholds, and with sea power in our hands, the invasion of Egypt from the East or North would be a well-nigh impossible enterprise. It was always a cause of surprise to me that we did not very early in the War seize and fortify the harbours of Haifa and Jaffa. This might easily have been done, as they were practically undefended, and the people were in their hearts pro-British. Even Gaza could have been occupied and fortified in the early days. With these three towns in our hands no Turkish force could have been organised in Palestine or used against Egypt. No army could possibly march down the maritime plain with these occupied towns menacing their flank, while the other route to Egypt by the eastward of the Jordan Valley is almost impossible for a large army.

Some eighty years ago Ibrahim Pasha was forced to retire to Egypt from Damascus by this eastern route because we held the coast ports. He left the ancient capital of Syria with some eighty thousand men, and, although he fought no battle on the way, his losses from sickness, hunger, thirst, and fatigue amounted to over sixty-five thousand men.

This gives one some little idea of the chance we missed in not making adequate use of our sea power by seizing the coast towns in the Levant during the Great War.

The physical conformation of Palestine adds enormously to its strategical strength.

The country is divided into four longitudinal belts running practically throughout the length of the country from North to South. Along the sea coast run the narrow maritime plains of Philistia, Sharon, and Acre. These narrow plains stretch from the borders of Egypt to the mountains of Lebanon.

The next belt of country consists of the continuation of the Lebanon range, which runs down practically unbroken through central Palestine, losing itself in the Southern Desert.

This hilly range constitutes the heart of the Holy Land and comprises the provinces of Galilee, Samaria, and Judæa. The only complete break in this range occurs between Galilee and Samaria, where the Plain of Esdraelon and the Valley of Jezreel cut right across and leave an open doorway from East to West. Through this gap from time immemorial armies have marched and counter-marched to and from Egypt.

The next belt of country is the great depression of the Jordan Valley, the deepest known in the world. It runs from "the waters of Merom," near the foothills of Hermon, where it is on a level with the Mediterranean, to the Dead Sea, where it is nearly 1,300 ft. below sea-level.

To the eastward of the Jordan Valley runs the table-land of the Hauran, Gilead, and Moab. This rich belt of territory is from twenty to sixty miles wide and ranges from 2,000 ft. to 4,000 ft. above sea-level. It loses itself to the South and East in the Arabian and Syrian Deserts.

The natural frontiers of Palestine are the Mediterranean on the West, the Syrian Desert to the East, the Arabian and Sinai Deserts to the South, and the difficult mountain passes of the Lebanon to the North. Next to the sea no better frontiers can be found than mountain passes and deserts.

It will therefore be seen that if Palestine is given anything like

81

her Biblical frontiers, troops could readily be placed on any threatened point and practically make the invasion of the country an impossibility.

As a matter of fact, a small national army in Palestine would make that country almost as impregnable as are the Cantons of Switzerland.

It is of the first importance to British interests to further the creation of a friendly State in Palestine which would act as a buffer between herself and any aggressive neighbour to the North or East.

The greatest soldiers and statesmen of the past realised that in order to obtain dominion over the East it was first of all necessary to secure the friendly co-operation of the people of Palestine.

Alexander the Great knew what a help to his Greek Empire of the East the Jews would be. He therefore showed them the greatest friendship, and allowed them every possible civil and religious liberty.

Later on, when Palestine came under the dominion of Rome, Julius Cæsar, the first and greatest of the Roman Emperors, realized so fully that without a friendly Palestine he could not hope to overthrow the Parthians and Persians to the eastward that in order to obtain the friendship of the Jews he freed Palestine from tribute, withdrew his legions from the country, exempted Jews from serving in the army, and allowed them full liberty of conscience, not only in Palestine but throughout the entire Empire.

Coming down to more modern times, we find Napoleon following as far as possible the policy of his two great predecessors. At one time, early in his career, he made an effort to restore the Jews to Palestine, and he would probably have been successful in his scheme, and made himself ruler of a French Empire in the East, only, unfortunately for him, Nelson, at the battle of the Nile, deprived him of the command of the sea. Nothing daunted by this, however, he marched his soldiers through the Sinai Desert and subdued practically all Palestine, but, owing to British sea-power, we were able to throw troops into Acre, and by his defeat at the famous siege of that place, Napoleon's eastern ambitions came to an end.

Great as was the importance of a friendly Palestine to the Greek and Roman Empires, a friendly Palestine to-day is of immensely more importance to the peace and prosperity of the British Empire. Our statesmen were, therefore, but following in the footsteps of the greatest men of the past when they issued the world-famous Balfour Declaration pledging England to use her best endeavours to establish a National Home in Palestine for the Jewish people.

It is useless to deny the fact that England is not nearly so popular in the Near East as she was thirty or forty years ago. The Egyptians have shown us pretty clearly that they have no love for us, while it is very evident that the Arab kingdoms have ambitions of their own in those regions, which might prove a very grave menace to our eastern communications. Naturally, Turkey—or what is left of that once great Empire—realises that it is to England that she owes her downfall, while the policy of Greece, at the moment at all events, also runs counter to our own.

It is very necessary, therefore, that Palestine should be colonised by a people whose interests will go hand in hand with those of England and who will readily grasp at union with the British Empire.

The Jews are the only people who fulfil these conditions. They have ever looked upon Palestine as their natural heritage, and although they were ruthlessly torn from it some two thousand years ago, yet through all the terrible years of their exile they have never lost the imperishable hope of a return to the Land of Promise. They have always had a friendly feeling for this country, and if England now deals justly with Israel, this friendly feeling will be increased tenfold. They would be quite unable to stand alone in Palestine for some time, and therefore their one aim and object would be to co-operate wholeheartedly with the Power that had not only reinstated them in their own land, but whose strong arm was adequate to protect them from the encroachments and aggressions of neighbouring states.

It will undoubtedly be their policy to walk hand in hand with England. British and Jewish interests are so similar and so interwoven that they fit into each other as the hand does the glove.

In short, when the long-expected Restoration of the Jewish people to the Promised Land becomes an accomplished fact, then the vital interests of the British Empire in those regions will be unassailable.

CHAPTER XX

HOSPITAL SCANDAL AT JERUSALEM

It will be remembered that I had been ordered to proceed to Nimrin to intercept any Turks who might attempt to break through from the South. When I reached my camp I found about 1,500 Turkish prisoners already concentrated there; hundreds of them were too feeble and ill to be marched further, but about 1,000 were considered fit enough to go on, and these were escorted by Captain Harris and a small detachment of the 38th to Jericho, and, after a short rest there, on to the prisoners' cage at Ludd.

On October 1st Battalion Headquarters moved to Jerusalem, and on the way thither it was pitiful to see these unfortunate Turkish prisoners, starving and sick, crawling at a snail's pace up the steep ascent from the Jordan Valley through the Judæan Wilderness; many fell by the way and died from sheer exhaustion. The medical arrangements were quite inadequate to cope even with our own sick, who now began to feel the effect of the poisonous Mellahah, and went down daily by scores.

Our new camp was situated about a mile outside the walls of Jerusalem to the southward, on the Hebron road, and by the time we reached it hundreds of the men, exhausted and worn out from the effects of their terrible experiences in the Jordan Valley, were ill with malaria; practically every officer also was struck down with the same fell disease. I myself had been far from well throughout the recent operations, but I managed, with the skilful aid of our Medical Officer, Captain Haldin Davis, to keep going.

Unfortunately, just before we arrived in Camp, there had been a terrific downpour of rain, which had thoroughly soaked the ground, and as there was no hospital accommodation available, the unfortunate patients had to lie on the wet earth, with only one blanket, and no medical comforts or treatment. There were no nurses or orderlies, and the men received no attention of any kind, except such as could be given by those of their comrades who were still able to move about. As a result of this lamentable state of affairs, which could easily have been prevented by a little forethought on the part of the Staff, many died of malaria and pneumonia, and one poor fellow killed himself by cutting his throat in his delirium.

Captain Davis had been taken ill at Nimrin, and removed in

an ambulance to hospital. I made urgent appeals for another doctor, but without avail, and it was nearly a whole year before the authorities thought it worth while to provide a medical officer for this Jewish Battalion, which at one time was almost 2,000 strong. Not only were the Jewish troops unable to find hospital accommodation, but hundreds of others also—British, Australian, New Zealand, and Indian.

The whole thing was a grave scandal, which must be laid at the door of the responsible muddlers.

It was distressing to see the German Hospice on the Mount of Olives, a building which was absolutely ideal for a Hospital, used for Staff purposes, while the sick and wounded men, who had suffered all the hardships and done all the fighting, were allowed to lie about on the wet ground in and around Jerusalem. The muddle was not the fault of the few medical men on the spot, for they worked like slaves. The whole of the blame for this wanton lack of organisation rests with G.H.Q. I had written in the previous July recommending that hospital accommodation should be provided at Jerusalem for Jewish troops, but no notice was taken of my recommendation. If this had been acted upon many deaths and much unnecessary suffering would have been avoided.

In my own battalion we lost over a score of men in this way, who, I am convinced, would not have died if proper hospital arrangements had been available, and had it not been for the timely arrival of Captain Salaman, R.A.M.C., with the 39th Battalion, to whom I turned over all my sick, the death-roll would in all probability have been much greater.

The battalion numbers, owing to the hardships we had undergone, were reduced from a strength of nearly 1,000 to about six officers and less than 150 men.

I can illustrate the pettiness of at least some of the G.H.Q. Staff no better than by giving the following correspondence.

It will be remembered that I had reported to General Allenby in the Jordan Valley that the medical arrangements were not good. This apparently displeased some of the Staff, for they hunted up a private telegram which I had sent some months previously (on July 18th), addressed to the Secretary, Medical Committee, Jewish Regiment, London, in which I had said:—

"You should see Sir Nevil Macready. Am strongly advising base to be at Jerusalem."

On discovering this mare's nest the D.A.G. sent the following memo. to General Chaytor:—

A. 13780.
Subject: Medical
Arrangements for
Jewish Battalions.

To General Chaytor,
Headquarters,
Chaytor's Force.

Please find attached herewith a copy of a telegram purporting to have been sent by the Officer Commanding 38th Royal Fusiliers.

Please call upon this officer to furnish his reasons and such explanation as he may have to offer for advising a course of action which concerns the C.-in-C. under whom he is serving, without reference to or obtaining permission from the C.-in-C.

(Signed)—Major-General, D.A.G.
G.H.Q. 1st Echelon,
17th September, 1918.

All this ado because I had simply sent a private telegram to the Jewish Hospital Committee months before to say I was advising a Hospital base to be set up at Jerusalem. This telegram was in reply to a cable from the Committee in London asking if special hospital accommodation could be provided for Jewish soldiers.

From the date on this memorandum it will be seen that G.H.Q. thought fit to send out such a communication on the very eve of the great advance. It would have been much more useful if the Deputy Adjutant General had devoted his attention to providing Hospital accommodation for the unfortunate sick and wounded, instead of choosing such a moment to harry troops in the field engaged in a great offensive, the success of which meant everything to England.

There was no excuse whatever for this memo., because on the 26th June, 1918, immediately on receipt of the cable from the Hospital Committee, I had sent the following to G.H.Q.:—

38th Battn. R.F.
No. A/412/1/3.
31st Inf. Brg. No. 57d.
10th Divn. No. 1324A.
XX. Corps No. P.C.A. 563.
G.H.Q. 1st Echelon No. a/13780.
Head Q. 31st. Inf. Brg.

I have received the following cable from the Hon. Sec. Medical Committee for Jewish Units:

"The Matron-in-Chief Q.A.I.M.N.S. sanctions Jewish Nursing Staff for Service in Palestine. Can you arrange Jewish wards in existing military Hospitals or other special provision? "Committee awaits reply."

With reference to the above cable I have to state that when I was organising the Jewish Units in England, I had recommended a Jewish Base Hospital, and the A.G., Sir N. Macready, had sanctioned this, and given instructions, after I left England for Egypt, that it was to be based at Plymouth.

The A.G. probably misunderstood my intention when he based it at Plymouth, as I had intended that the Hospital should be based in Egypt or Palestine. I therefore wrote home and suggested that there was no need for a special Jewish Hospital in England.

I have no doubt that the above cable is the result of some negotiation with the A.G., and I would suggest that this matter be referred to G.H.Q., 1st Echelon, so that they may get into touch with the W.O., and find out what has been decided upon in this question. Personally I would recommend that the Hospital should be at Jerusalem.

(Signed) J. H. Patterson, Lt.-Colonel,
Commanding 38th Battn., R.F.
In the Field, 26/6/18.

To the above I received the following reply:

A/13780.

Subject: Jewish Wards,
and Military Hospitals.
H.Q. 20TH Corps.

With reference to your memo. No. P.C.A. 565, dated 30/6/18, and attached correspondence regarding the question of Jewish wards in Military Hospitals. All Jewish soldiers will be sent to one particular Ward in the 27th General Hospital, as long as the casualty rate allows of this procedure being followed.

(Signed) F. Dalrymple, Lt.-Colonel,
A.A.G. for D.A.G.
G.H.Q., 1st Echelon,
10/7/18.

It will be seen therefore that if the D.A.G. had only known what was going on in his own office there would have been no need for him to trump up this petty inquisition, or trouble anybody for an explanation about a private telegram which had been sent to London a couple of months previously. General Chaytor had the good sense to retain the D.A.G.'s memo, until active operations were over, upon which he sent it on to me. As an explanation had to be given, the following is a copy of my reply:

> *Headquarters,*
> *Chaytor's Force.*
>
> *A/412/1/3.*
>
>   *With reference to your M.C.412 dated 13/10/18 re medical arrangements for Jewish Battalions, I think that perhaps it will explain the situation if I point out that I was in direct touch with the War Office on all questions affecting the Jewish Battalions, and I had several interviews with Sir Nevil Macready on matters relating to this Jewish movement; in fact, I was looked upon in England as the responsible leader, and I had every conceivable kind of case to investigate and decide. I had already told Sir Nevil Macready my views while in England re Hospital for Jewish soldiers, and when I got a cable from this unofficial medical committee I replied in a private cable recommending them to consult him, and stating my own private views on the question.*
>
>   *I certainly do not consider this private expression of opinion as "advising a course of action," and when I sent the cable nothing was further from my mind. I simply referred the Committee to Sir Nevil Macready, with whom I had already discussed the matter, and said what I personally thought the best place for a base.*
>
>   *Naturally no action could be taken without consulting the C.-in-C., E.E.F.; as a matter of fact I did forward a copy of this telegram to G.H.Q., and also a letter in which I recommended Jerusalem as a base.*
>
>   *I attach copy of my letter and, at the same time, I regret that my advice re Hospital at Jerusalem was not taken. If a Jewish Hospital had been established there, before the recent operations took place, much unnecessary suffering and many deaths would have been avoided. Men of the Jewish Battalions, who were very ill indeed, were lying about in hundreds on wet ground in Jerusalem, because there was no room for them in the overcrowded hospitals, and it was quite impossible to get our sick evacuated for days after they had really become cot cases.*

It was no fault of the Medical Officers on the spot; it was simply impossible to cope with the sick for want of Medical Officers and hospital accommodation. I may mention that of the Battalion under my command alone there are 27 Officers and 824 other ranks in hospital, as a result of the Jordan Valley and subsequent operations.

In conclusion I must say I am somewhat surprised that a private communication which I sent to a private individual in July last should be produced at this stage.

I again and most emphatically state that I advised no course of action, merely gave my private opinion, and had no idea of any such action when I sent the cable.

(Signed) J. H. Patterson, Lt.-Colonel,
Commanding 38th Battn. Royal Fusiliers.

In the Field,
19/10/18.

As a result of the representations made by the Medical Committee in England on behalf of the Jewish Battalions, a Staff of Jewish Nurses, in charge of Sister Oppenheimer, were sent out to the 27th General Hospital at Abbasieh, near Cairo, and I have on many occasions heard expressions of gratitude showered on these nurses by men who had been under their care.

It will be remembered that a number of Palestinian Jewish ladies volunteered for Nursing Service as soon as the British occupied Jaffa and Jerusalem. I had strongly urged that their offer of service should be accepted and that they should be taken on and trained, for I foresaw that they would be required as soon as a determined effort to oust the Turk from Palestine was made.

Unfortunately, my advice was not taken, for, as I have already shown, they were sadly needed in Jerusalem.

Later on about half-a-dozen Jewish ladies, including the Misses Berline, who were well known in Jaffa and Jerusalem, were enrolled and attached to the General Hospital at Belah. I went there on more than one occasion to see my men, and on enquiring from the Matron-in-Charge how the Jewish nurses were getting on she told me that she had never had better or more conscientious workers under her in all her experience.

It was deplorable that the Staff had ignored the voluntary offer of the Jewish ladies until it was almost too late to make use of their services.

CHAPTER XXI

LIFE AT LUDD

On the 9th October the battered remnant of the battalion moved from Jerusalem to Ludd by rail, where it was taken on the strength of Lines of Communication troops for garrison duties.

When we heard that we were to be severed from the Anzacs our feeling was one of regret, for every individual in the battalion had the greatest admiration, respect, and affection for General Chaytor and his Staff, and, in fact, a feeling of real comradeship for every officer and man in the Anzac Mounted Division.

My sick and ailing could not even yet be taken into Hospital owing to lack of accommodation, so I left them attached to the 39th Battalion, under the care of Captain Salaman, R.A.M.C.

Our transport had been ordered to proceed from Jerusalem to Ludd by road on the 5th October, but as the animals were worn to mere skin and bone by hard work, and nearly all the drivers were down with malaria, I represented to the authorities that it would be impossible for them to move for at least a week, so they remained in Jerusalem for some days after Battalion Headquarters had left the City.

When eventually the transport marched in to Ludd I found both animals and men in a most pitiable condition. One of my best N.C.O.s, Corporal Lloyd, was delirious with fever, and several other men who should have gone into Hospital at Jerusalem but were unable to gain admission were brought down on the wagons. All these I sent into the local Hospital; Corporal Lloyd unfortunately did not recover, and died soon after he was admitted. Of the half-dozen officers who had so far escaped the malaria, one after another went down and were carried off to Hospital, until, out of the whole battalion, only Captain Leadley, Lieutenant Bullock, and myself were left in Camp!

Major Neill was one of the last to succumb, and his attack was so severe that his life was despaired of. He was on the "dangerously ill" list for some time, but fortunately recovered.

Day after day the few remaining men we had left went to hospital until, in the end, I was put to such straits that I had to appeal once more to the Australians, who had a reinforcement camp near us under the command of Major Ferguson. I rode over and told him the difficulty I had in finding men even to feed my animals, and asked him to spare me a score of troopers to help with the exercising, watering, and grooming, etc., of the transport animals.

As usual, the Australians were all out to help, and readily gave me all the assistance I asked for.

Soon after the 38th Battalion left Jerusalem, Colonel Margolin also received orders to proceed to Ludd, although it was well known that hundreds of sick were in the camp. What would have happened to these unfortunate sufferers if he had obeyed orders and marched away leaving them to their fate, sick and helpless as they were, I shall leave the reader to imagine. Luckily for these poor fellows Colonel Margolin refused to leave until such time as they could be accommodated in Hospital.

Eventually he succeeded in getting his men into medical wards, and then he and what was left of his battalion came and camped within a mile of us at Surafend, a village between Ludd and Jaffa.

On the evening of the 22nd October Colonel Margolin and Captain Salaman rode into my camp and complained to me of the discrimination and unfair treatment to which the Jewish soldiers were being subjected in the Hospitals—giving me various instances to illustrate certain of their statements.

As the Senior Officer of the Jewish Battalions, not being myself a Jew, I was deeply hurt at the un-English methods adopted towards men who had done so well in the field in England's cause, and felt that I would not be doing my duty to those under my command, and to Jewry generally, unless I protested against this unfair discrimination.

I considered that the best way of bringing matters to a head was by requesting to be relieved of my command as a protest against the anti-Jewish policy which prevailed. I accordingly sent forward my resignation. This found its way to G.H.Q., but as certain individuals there had no desire to see me land unmuzzled in England, my resignation was not accepted. Some of the Staff knew only too well that if I were free to return to England I would at once let the authorities there know that their representatives in Palestine were not carrying out the declared policy of the Imperial Government, but, on the contrary, were doing their best to make of the Balfour Declaration a mere "scrap of paper."

As G.H.Q. was then only some two miles from my Camp I thought it might help matters if I could see Major-General Louis Jean Bols, the Chief-of-Staff, and get him to put a stop to the persecution that was going on, and see that his underlings "played the game." I therefore called on this gentleman, but he, for reasons best known to himself, refused to see me.

I told his A.D.C. that I was camped close by and would be glad to see the General any time that was convenient to him, but I left his office feeling there never would be a convenient time, and so, in fact, it turned out.

When my resignation was refused and my request for an interview treated in the same manner, I made a vigorous protest against the anti-Jewish policy which prevailed, and stated that if it was not altered I would have the matter placed before the Secretary of State for War in Parliament.

As a result of this I got a letter from G.H.Q. requesting me to furnish a list of the complaints I wished to make, and also asking me to forward recommendations for the improvement and comfort of the Jewish Battalion.

In my reply I pointed out how the battalion had suffered owing to the discrimination to which it had been subjected, and gave specific instances of unfair and unjust treatment during our service with the E.E.F.

I also forwarded a separate memorandum recommending various changes for the improvement and comfort of the men. I made five specific suggestions; not a single one of these was carried out.

One of my suggestions was that a special Jewish name and badge should be given to the battalion. This had been promised by the War Office, but the fact that it was granted was purposely withheld from our knowledge by the Staff, and it was only by accident, a whole year later, that I discovered this deliberate shelving of Army Council Orders by G.H.Q. in Egypt.

This could not have been an oversight because I had written more than once to enquire whether this distinction had yet been conferred on the battalion.

Having seen the majority of my officers and men all carried off to Hospital, and feeling ill and depressed in my lonely camp, I sat down late one night and wrote a letter of condolence to Mrs. Cross. I told her that although we had wired to every Turkish Hospital, from Es Salt to Damascus, we could obtain no information about her husband; I wound up my letter by stating that although there might still be some very faint hope, she must steel herself to face the facts, for I feared she would never see her husband again.

It must have been close on midnight when I lay down, and, as I was unable to sleep, I was reading by the dim light of a candle when suddenly I saw a white ghostly face appear in the tent door, and only that I knew Cross was dead I would have thought it was the face of Cross. Then a sepulchral voice said, "Are you awake, Sir?" and I began to wonder if it were all a dream. When the figure approached the light, I saw that it really was Cross, so I bounded up to give him a welcome—such a welcome as one would give to a friend who had risen from the dead.

It appeared that when the patrol had been ambushed, Cross got wounded and lay under a sandbank where he was discovered by the Turks; they carried him off, and, as they were then retiring as fast as they could, took him with them, pushed him on to Amman, and from there by rail to Damascus. He was about to be sent further north when the British entered the city. In the confusion Cross made good his escape and eventually worked his way back to me. Thus it was that nobody knew anything of his whereabouts, for he had never reported to any of the Hospitals en route.

Mrs. Cross had already been informed by the War Office that he was missing and reported killed. I told Cross that I had just posted a letter to his wife to say that I feared that he must have been killed: he, of course, at once sent a private cable to tell her that he was alive and well, while I sent an official one to the War Office giving the same account. At all events, my letter of condolence to Mrs. Cross will always be a good souvenir of the part her husband took in the Great War.

CHAPTER XXII

AT RAFA

The Armistice with Turkey was announced on the 31st October, 1918, amid the firing of guns and rockets and joy stunts by the Air Force above our camp at Ludd.

On the 6th November the battalion was ordered to proceed to Rafa to recuperate, refit and reorganise, and on the 7th, in the early morning, we arrived at this frontier station bordering on "the desert and the town."

Rafa is actually in Egypt, just over the borders of Palestine, on the Palestine-Egyptian Railway line some five miles from the Mediterranean, and here the tents of Israel were pitched.

93

Along the whole coast in this neighbourhood there runs a belt, about four miles deep, of sand dunes and sand hills. These are very irregular in outline, running in some places to peaks nearly 100 feet in height, and in others forming miniature precipices, valleys and gullies. It is, in fact, a mountainous country on a lilliputian scale.

The sand is so firm that a horse can be ridden all over it, thereby giving great joy to the hunters of the jackals and hyenas which roam on its barren surface. The air on this stretch of sandy dunes is wonderfully fresh and exhilarating, and we drank it in with delight after our trying experience in the Jordan Valley. The seashore itself abounds with millions of curious shells.

The sand belt ends abruptly landwards and, at the very edge of it, the Bedouin scratches up the soil with an antiquated plough which dates from the time of Abraham. Green waving crops, pleasant to the eye, may be seen almost under the shadow of a sand cliff. The country inland consists of a somewhat sandy soil and gently undulating plains which are, for the greater part, cultivated by Arabs who live in scattered villages, and by Bedouins who come and go as the spirit moves them. The whole place is honeycombed with holes burrowed by the little conies, which makes riding at a fast pace somewhat hazardous.

Such was the quiet little spot in which we found ourselves after our strenuous and exciting days in the Jordan Valley and the Land of Gilead. Day by day our men gradually came back from Hospital and, owing to drafts from the 40th Battalion, our strength was soon over 30 officers and 1,500 other ranks.

After a brief time for rest, we took over "Line of Communication" duties, and found ourselves with many miles of railway and country to safeguard. Our life now became one constant round of guards, escorts, fatigues, and drills whenever a few men could be spared from other duties for the latter purpose. There were thousands of prisoners of war in our custody, as well as a huge captured Turkish ammunition depot, supply stores, engineer park, and all kinds of workshops, etc., etc.

Soon after we got to Rafa I lost the services of Captain Leadley, M.C., who was demobilized at his own request and returned to England. I selected to succeed him Captain Duncan Sandison—as stubborn a Scot as ever wore a kilt, a first-rate officer, loyal to the core, and a great favourite with everybody except the evil-doers.

Early in December I received another large draft of raw Jewish recruits from the 40th Battalion Royal Fusiliers—all American citizens.

I strongly objected to these untrained men being sent to me

94

under the circumstances in which I was placed, for it was impossible to give them any training owing to the excessive duties we were called upon to perform day and night. I knew that the result of putting raw recruits to fulfil duties which should have been carried out only by seasoned soldiers, must, before very long, end in disaster. I foresaw endless breaches of discipline, not because the men were evilly disposed, but because they were untrained and knew nothing of military discipline.

I accordingly urged the Staff to remove all these recruits, of whom I had about 800, to a training centre, and repeatedly warned the authorities of what the result must be if this were not done, but not the slightest notice was taken of my appeal.

It was a thousand pities that these enthusiastic American volunteers did not get a fair chance to show their mettle. I well remember how favourably I was impressed with their physique and general appearance when I inspected them on their arrival at Rafa. They were miles ahead, physically, of the men who joined the battalion in England—in fact I do not believe that there was a unit in the whole of the E.E.F. that held such a fine-looking body of men. Because they were untrained and had no idea of discipline, these hefty youths were constantly in trouble for committing breaches of military rules and regulations. They simply did not understand soldiering or what it meant. In this way I got to know the majority of them fairly well. We had many interesting meetings at "office hour." Of course, in dealing with these volunteers, I never forgot that the faults they were guilty of were, in great measure, due to lack of training, and I dealt with them accordingly. Their military offences were not grave, just the delinquencies that must be expected of recruits, because they are recruits.

Nevertheless, it is always a danger to have a battalion, supposed to be at any moment ready to take the field, swamped with some 800 raw untrained men.

I felt so strongly on this question, and so clearly foresaw the inevitable end, that having failed to move the authorities myself, I cast about me to see where I could look for help and sympathy in the difficult situation in which I was placed; the only possible man who might be able to do something was the Acting-Chairman of the Zionist Commission then in Palestine. It will be remembered that, soon after the famous Balfour Declaration, Dr. Weizmann, the President of the Zionist Organisation, was sent out at the head of a Commission to investigate conditions and safeguard Jewish interests in Palestine. Dr. Weizmann was received by H.M. the King before his departure from England, and came out armed with strong letters from the Prime Minister and Mr. Balfour to General Allenby.

95

Dr. Weizmann spent some time doing useful work in Palestine, and was then recalled to England in connection with the Zionist policy then before our Government. The mantle of Dr. Weizmann eventually fell on Dr. Eder, and to him I now applied myself, as it was a matter of the greatest importance that no undeserved slur should fall upon the Jewish Battalion.

Like myself, however, Dr. Eder was unable to effect anything.

I felt very strongly that the whole attitude adopted towards the Jewish Battalions was unworthy of British traditions of fair play. It is of course possible that General Allenby did not know of the treatment to which we were subjected by certain members of his Staff and other underlings, for naturally only the greater questions would come before him. If he had known he would surely never have countenanced the jeopardising of the good name of any battalion in the E.E.F. by swamping it with over 800 raw recruits who, owing to the "exigencies of the service," had to be put on trained soldiers' duties the moment they joined.

Unfortunately I was unable to let him know of our dilemma, for the Chief of Staff, Major-General Louis Jean Bols, had forbidden me to address the Commander-in-Chief direct, and apparently the appeals which I had made on this question never reached a sympathetic quarter.

As I have already said, I had been ill from the time we began operations in the Jordan Valley and was now reduced to a skeleton, but by careful dieting I had hoped to weather the storm and had so far managed to keep out of Hospital.

Thinking that a few days change would improve my health I applied for leave and went to Cairo. While I was there I happened by chance to meet Captain Salaman in the street, and he was so shocked at my appearance that he straightway convoyed me off to Nasrieh Hospital, where I was taken in hand by Captain Wallace, R.A.M.C. In a couple of weeks he had me well enough to be transferred to the beautiful Convalescent Home at Sirdariah, where the matron and staff of nurses were kindness and consideration personified; a short spell in this well-managed institution completed my cure, at the end of which I rejoined the battalion.

CHAPTER XXIII

RETURN OF THE ANZACS

About this time the battalion was inspected by the G.O.C. Lines of Communication, and the following is what he wrote of the impression we made on him:

HEADQUARTERS,

PALESTINE LINES OF COMMUNICATION,

8th January, 1919.

I was very glad to inspect your battalion and I was much struck with the soldierly appearance presented by the men.

(Signed) E. W. Broadbent,
General Officer Commanding P.L. of C.

Isolated as we were on the edge of the desert we found life at Rafa somewhat dull and dreary. Sandstorms were the bane of one's life there; a "Khamsin" or hot wind would blow for days at a time, enveloping the place in a cloud of fine sand and making life one long misery while it lasted. One's eyes, nose, and throat got choked up, while every morsel of food was full of grit. "Khamsin" is Arabic for fifty; the hot wind is supposed to blow for that number of days but, thank Heaven, it rarely lasted more than a week on end at Rafa.

There were no other troops in the place to vary the deadly monotony. True, there were some Engineers of the Railway Operating Division, but we found them somewhat selfish, for although they had an excellent Concert Hall they refused our Concert Party permission to use it. Even at Rafa the few underlings on the Staff took their cue from above and did what they could to make our life as uncomfortable as possible, until they came to know us better.

It can be imagined, therefore, with what joyful feelings we saw our old friends of the Anzac Division march into Rafa and make it their headquarters.

Since we had parted from the Anzacs in Gilead we had seen nothing of them, but we knew that they had been camped in the green fields and pleasant pastures surrounding the Jewish Colony of

Richon-le-Zion. The slings and arrows of misfortunes removed them from these sylvan surroundings, but whatever ill wind blew them to Rafa it was a godsend for us.

In these piping days of Peace, now that we were among our old friends once more, there was horse-racing, hunting, tournaments and boxing galore, while an enterprising kinema man came and photographed camp scenes and groups of officers and men.

In the sand dunes around Rafa many ancient coins were to be found, and General Chaytor himself could always be relied on to head a hunt for these and other relics of antiquity. We never failed to find some objects of interest—bits of glazed pottery, glass, beads, pins, bangles, rings, etc. Every time there was a storm the top sand would get blown away and we could always go and make fresh finds in the ground we had already explored, and great was the competition as to who should discover the best specimens.

The General had the eye of a lynx for such things, and it was rarely indeed that anyone else had a look in while he was to the fore. He discovered some very beautiful old mosaics buried at Shellal, and these he had carefully sketched and artistically coloured, exactly as they were in the original. I was very pleased when he kindly presented me with a copy.

The rolling downs round about us were dotted here and there with the graves of fallen Australian and New Zealand soldiers, and, riding as I often did with General Chaytor, he would explain the operations which took place when the British first entered Palestine at this point. He gave me many vivid descriptions of the part which his Brigade had taken in the overthrow of the Turks at the Battle of Rafa.

The General had a very narrow escape on that occasion. In the middle of the battle, when he was galloping from one position to another, attended only by his orderly, he came suddenly upon a concealed trench full of Turks. Fortunately they thought he was at the head of a Squadron, so threw up their hands and surrendered. The General left his orderly to march off the prisoners and galloped on to conduct the fight elsewhere.

We motored over to Gaza once and spent a most interesting day there.

From Ali Muntar, a hill to the east of the town, which had been the General's headquarters in the first battle of Gaza, he described the whole situation. From this point almost every bit of Gaza and the surrounding country could easily be seen.

It will be remembered that at the first battle we claimed a victory which history has not since been able to verify, for we retired in hot haste on Rafa; but it is said that, if there had only been a little more push and go in the high command that day, Gaza would have been ours.

As a matter of fact it was ours at one time, for part of General Chaytor's brigade was right in the town, where they captured some hundreds of prisoners and a couple of guns which they turned on the Turks in Gaza with considerable effect, sighting their strange new pieces at point blank range by peeping through the bore of the guns.

The Turks were everywhere beginning to throw up the sponge, when, alas, the British Force was suddenly ordered to retire because a Turkish relieving column was seen approaching in the distance; but if only the British Division, which all this time had been held in reserve, had been thrust forward to intercept this column, tired, thirsty, and done up as it was, we could, no doubt, have shattered it and won a complete victory.

General Chaytor was ordered to retire somewhat early in the afternoon, but, as he had a squadron right in the town, and many wounded men in advanced positions, he waited until nightfall before withdrawing, taking with him all his wounded, and also the Turkish prisoners and captured guns. No matter who had the "wind up" that day, it certainly was not General Chaytor or his Brigade.

The second battle of Gaza was, of course, a terrible fiasco, in which we were repulsed and lost thousands of men to no purpose.

On another occasion I motored, with Colonel Croll, R.A.M.C., of the Anzacs, to Beersheba. It was at this point that General Allenby made a successful thrust when he first took command in Palestine, and from that day to this he has never looked back. The Anzacs and the Australian Mounted Division in this attack made a wide turning movement, outflanked Beersheba, burst suddenly in upon Tel el Saba, some three miles to the east of it, galloped the Turkish trenches, and poured into Beersheba at one end in a whirlwind of dust and storm while the Turks skedaddled out of it as fast as ever they could run from the other end, and made for the shelter of the foothills towards Hebron.

The New Zealanders say that they were responsible for the capture of Tel el Saba, for it was they who outflanked it; while the Australians assured me that it was they who had stormed it at a mad gallop. At all events it was a decisive victory for the Australians and New Zealanders (for both took part in it), and as fine a piece of mounted work as had been done so far during the war. Dash, energy, and initiative were shown in a very high degree by all ranks engaged.

99

In the little cemetery at Beersheba I visited the grave of Major Markwell, one of the bravest officers who fell that day.

We also paid a visit to the site of Old Beersheba, and were greatly interested in peering down into the well dug at this celebrated place by the Patriarch Abraham.

From Beersheba we motored to Gaza along the former Turkish front; every inch of the way had been fortified and turned into a maze of trenches, with formidable redoubts here and there throughout the line.

Once Beersheba was captured, the heart was taken out of the Turkish resistance, though they put up some stiff fighting before they were dislodged, especially at Atawineh, a strong redoubt near the centre of the position.

After the capture of Beersheba, Lieutenant-Colonel S. F. Newcombe, D.S.O., R.E., dashed northwards with part of the Camel Corps, to cut off the Turks retreating on the Beersheba-Hebron Road. He reached a point within a few miles of the latter place, but was surrounded by six battalions of the enemy. He held out gallantly for three days; but at last, when he had exhausted all his ammunition and suffered heavy casualties, he was obliged to surrender.

Fate holds in its lap many surprises. If Colonel Newcombe had not been captured that day he would undoubtedly, with ordinary luck, have won distinction and rank, but there was another and better prize awaiting him at Constantinople, for, while he was a prisoner and convalescing in that city, he met a charming young lady who, at great personal risk, helped him to escape from the clutches of the Turk, and afterwards became his wife.

CHAPTER XXIV

A RED-LETTER DAY

Soon after the Anzac Division came to Rafa, General Chaytor expressed a wish to inspect the battalion and present decorations to those officers, N.C.O.s, and men who had won them while under his command.

It was a gloriously sunny afternoon, and every available man in the battalion was on parade when General Chaytor, accompanied by Colonel Bruxner and Major Anderson, rode on to the review ground and took the "General Salute."

The battalion was then formed up on three sides of a square; the officers, N.C.O.s, and men to be decorated stood in the centre, and as each was called out to have the coveted honour pinned to his breast, his deeds were recounted to the assembled troops.

Captain T. B. Brown won the Military Cross and bar for having gallantly led many a dangerous reconnaissance into the enemy's lines.

Lieutenant Fligelstone was also decorated with the Military Cross for good, gallant, and dangerous work successfully performed while he was acting as machine-gun officer.

Lieutenant Cameron and Lieutenant Bullock both won Military Crosses and bars for good and gallant patrol and intelligence work in the Jordan Valley.

Corporal Bloom, Lance-Corporal Elfman, and Privates Angel and Robinson were all decorated with the Military Medal for various gallant acts performed in the Mellahah, and during the recent operations.

Major Neill had the D.S.O. conferred on him for his able handling of the battalion while it was under his command in "Patterson's Column," Captain Leadley received the Military Cross for his good Staff work, and Company Sergeant-Major Plant won the D.C.M. for special services rendered by him during the whole time we were in the fighting line.

At the end of the presentation the General made the following address:

Colonel Patterson, Officers, N.C.O.s, and men of the 38th Jewish Battalion Royal Fusiliers, I have specially come here to-day, first of all to present decorations to the officers and men who have won them in the recent operations under my command.

Secondly, I want to tell you how sorry I am that I was not able to put you in the Van in the advance on Es Salt. I wished that you had been there, and I wanted you to be there, but the Indian Infantry and other units were in a more favourable position from which to spring off, while you were still entangled miles to the northward in the heavy sandhills of the Jordan Valley. In any case, even had you been in the Van you would have seen but little fighting, for the mounted men got well to the front and were able to effect the capture of Es Salt and Amman before the Infantry could possibly come up.

I am pleased to be able to tell you, however, that I was particularly struck with your good work on the Mellahah front, and by your gallant capture of the Umm esh Shert Ford and defeat of the Turkish rearguard when I gave you the order to go, for I was then enabled to push my mounted men over the Jordan at that crossing, and so you contributed materially to the capture of Es Salt and of the guns and other material which fell to our share; to the capture of Amman; the cutting of the Hedjaz Railway, and the destruction of the 4th Turkish Army, which helped considerably towards the great victory won at Damascus.

I briefly thanked the General for his praise of the battalion, and a march past the decorated officers and men concluded the pleasant ceremony. It was indeed a Red-Letter Day for the battalion.

It will be seen from the above what really good work was done by the Jewish Battalion, and how much it was appreciated by the one man who was in a position to judge of our fighting abilities by actual experience in the field.

Yet all mention of Jewish Troops was deliberately suppressed by the Staff at G.H.Q. True, Jewish Troops were mentioned in official despatches all over the world, but the part of these despatches relating to Jewish Troops was never allowed to appear in the Palestinian and Egyptian papers. This naturally upset and humiliated both Jewish troops and the Jewish population generally, for it gave outsiders the impression that we had failed to do our duty, whereas, on the contrary, the Jewish Battalion had done extraordinarily good work for England. It would, therefore, have been only mere justice and fair play if it had received recognition in the local Egyptian and Palestinian Press, but it was rigidly excluded from all mention by what the Times truthfully branded as "the most incompetent, the most inept, and the most savagely ruthless censorship in any country under British control."

This omission was especially noted by all when the Commander-in-Chief in his speech at Cairo, in December, 1918, mentioned all nationalities who fought under his command, including Armenians and West Indians, but maintained a stony silence on the doings of Jewish Troops in Palestine. Coming on the top of all our persecution, this was most marked.

The following is indeed in his despatch published in England, which must by some fluke or other have dodged the Censor:

GENERAL ALLENBY'S DESPATCH,
31st October, 1918.
In operations east of the Jordan.

The enemy, however, still held the bridgeheads on the west bank, covering the crossings of the Jordan at Umm es Shert, etc.

Early in the morning of the 22nd September, the 38th Battalion Royal Fusiliers captured the bridgehead at Umm es Shert.

Of the fighting troops, all have taken their share and have carried out what was required of them.

I will bring to notice the good fighting qualities shown by the newer units. These include ... the 38th and 39th (Jewish) Battalions of the Royal Fusiliers.

(Signed) E. H. H. Allenby, General,
Commander-in-Chief, E.E.F.

The Commander-in-Chief also wrote in reply to a letter of congratulation which he received from the Secretary of the Zionist Organization of America:

22d November, 1918.

DEAR SIR,
I have the honour to acknowledge your letter....
You will be glad to hear that the Jewish Regiment did consistently good work....

I received letters of congratulations from many prominent people, but the most valued of all was from that wonderful and truly great man, Theodore Roosevelt. I only received this letter, written three weeks before his lamented death, towards the end of March— over two months after he had passed away. It had been sent to France in error, and wandered in and out amongst the different armies there until somebody noticed that it had "E.E.F." on the address, and sent it on to Palestine:

11th December, 1918.

My dear Colonel Patterson,

I most heartily congratulate you on leading in what was not only one of the most important, but one of the most dramatic incidents in the whole War. To have the sons of Israel smite Ammon "hip and thigh" under your leadership is something worth while.

As for my own loss, the death of my son Quentin was very bitter, but it would have been far more bitter if he had been a hand's breadth behind his friends in entering the war. Two of my other sons have been wounded, one of them crippled. The other wounded one has recovered, and as Lieutenant-Colonel is now commanding his regiment on the march towards the Rhine. Kermit is Captain of Artillery, having first served in Mesopotamia, and then under Pershing in the Argonne fight.

With hearty congratulations,
Faithfully yours,
T. Roosevelt.

Although the Staff denied us any local credit, our Zionist friends in the country knew what good work the battalion had done, and we were glad to receive the following official letter from the Zionist Commission:

Zionist Commission to Palestine,
c/o Chief Political Officer,
G.H.Q., Tel-Aviv, Jaffa, Palestine,

15th October, 1918.

Colonel J. H. Patterson, D.S.O.,
38th R.F.

Dear Colonel Patterson,

It gives us great pleasure to express to you and to the men under your command of the 38th and 39th Royal Fusiliers, on behalf of the Zionist Commission, our warmest congratulations on the successful part taken by the Royal Fusiliers in the last battle that brought about the liberation of the rest of Palestine. We have always followed with the keenest interest the doings of the Regiment, and we are proud to know that it has done bravely and well.

At a meeting of the Zionist Commission held yesterday, Lieutenant Jabotinsky informed us of the distinctions conferred upon four of the men of your battalion. It was resolved at this meeting to congratulate you thereon and ask you to be good enough to convey the congratulations of the Commission to the men who had earned these distinctions.

With our best wishes for your welfare and that of the officers and men under your command,

I am, dear Colonel Patterson,
Yours faithfully,
(Signed) Jack Mosseri,
Secretary.

Soon after my return to England I received the following letter from General Chaytor, which will, I know, fill the hearts of the old boys of the 38th with pride:

Wellington,
New Zealand,
9th March, 1920.

My dear Patterson,

I hope the history of the 38th Battalion is out by now. So few people have heard of the battalion's good work, or of the very remarkable fact that in the operations that we hope have finally reopened Palestine to the Jews a Jewish force was fighting on the Jordan, within a short distance of where their forefathers, under Joshua, first crossed into Palestine, and all who hear about it are anxious to hear more.

I shall always be grateful to you and your battalion for your good work while with me in the Jordan Valley.

The way you smashed up the Turkish rearguard when it tried to counter-attack across the Jordan made our subsequent advance up the hills of Moab an easy matter.

With best wishes, yours sincerely,
(Signed) E. W. C. Chaytor.

CHAPTER XXV

JEWISH SOLDIERS ARE FORBIDDEN TO ENTER THE HOLY CITY

On the 24th February, 1919, I was appointed to the command of "Rafa Area." The "Area" was rather an extensive one; it included nearly the whole of the Sinai Desert to the south, and Palestine to the north, almost as far as Bir Salem, while to the east it went beyond Beersheba to the Arabian Desert. There were over 150 miles of railway to guard, and the Bedouins had to be constantly watched and checked, or they would have played all sorts of pranks with the line. Constant patrols had to be maintained, and every day provided a fresh problem for solution. The fresh-water pipe line from Egypt ran alongside the railway and, of course, the wandering and thirsty

105

Ishmaelite thought nothing of smashing this in order to get a drink for himself and his camel. We had to be on the alert all the time and nip these little enterprises of our friendly Allies in the bud. They did not hesitate to attempt to loot the supply stores of flour, forage, etc., stored at Rafa, and our sentries had many lively little encounters with these marauders, and I must say that the wily rascals took their chance of a bullet quite casually. While the Anzac Division was with us I felt quite easy in my mind about being able to keep these slippery customers in check, but it was quite "another pair of shoes" when the Anzacs were hurriedly called away to suppress the disorders in Egypt.

In addition to the 38th Battalion, I had some Indian Infantry holding Gaza, and some South African troops holding El Arish. As demobilization progressed these were withdrawn and the whole of this great area was, in the end, solely garrisoned and guarded by the Jewish Battalion. They performed their arduous duties extraordinarily well. They were scattered up and down the line in small posts, often in the midst of Arab villages and Bedouin camps, yet there was never any friction between Jew and Arab, although here was a likely setting for it, if there had been any real ill-feelings animating either side; but, as a matter of fact, the Jew and Arab got on wonderfully well together all over Palestine, and had worked amicably side by side for over forty years in the Jewish colonies.

When the Egyptian Nationalist riots started the Military Governor of El Arish feared an outbreak in this large Arab town, so I had to send reinforcements to the garrison there under the command of Captain Jaffe, an officer of the battalion. Aeroplanes flew up from the Aerodrome at Heliopolis, and swooping low over El Arish put the fear of the Lord into the inhabitants; this demonstration, and the great personal influence of the Military Governor, Colonel Parker, kept these people quiet, and they gave us no trouble whatever.

Later on we had to guard a number of political prisoners who were sent up from Egypt as a result of the disturbances there, and this added considerably to the heavy work of the battalion.

At Rafa there was an enormous Ammunition Depôt, covering acres of ground, and this was a constant source of anxiety, and had to be guarded on all sides, night and day. While the Jewish troops held it in custody nothing untoward happened, but, after they were removed, by some evil chance the whole place was blown up with considerable loss of life.

Notwithstanding the heavy work exacted from the battalion, there was one great consolation for the men. No petty discrimination could now be practised against them within my jurisdiction, and although I had five Staff Officers under my command, I found them quite good fellows, and willing to do all in their power to do the right thing by the Jewish troops.

Discrimination against Jews was, however, still shown in other quarters. Early in April the men were considerably upset on the receipt of orders from G.H.Q. that no Jewish soldier would be allowed to enter Jerusalem during the Passover; the order ran thus:

"The walled city (of Jerusalem) is placed out of bounds to all Jewish soldiers from the 14th to the 22nd April, inclusive."

I cannot conceive a greater act of provocation to Jewish soldiers than this, or a greater insult. The days during which they were prohibited from entering Jerusalem were the days of the Passover. Think of it! Jewish soldiers for the first time in their lives in Palestine and barred from the Temple Wall of Jerusalem during Passover! Only a Jew can really understand what it meant to these men, and the great strain it put on their discipline and loyalty.

How provocative and insulting this order was will be better understood when it is realized that the majority of the population of Jerusalem is Jewish, and, therefore, there could have been no possible reason for excluding Jewish troops belonging to a British unit, while other British troops were freely admitted, more especially as the conduct of the Jewish soldiers was, at all times, exemplary.

Not since the days of the Emperor Hadrian had such a humiliating decree been issued.

However, to make up somewhat for the action of the authorities, I made arrangements for the Passover to be observed at Rafa with all the joy and ceremony usually attending that great Feast of the Jewish People. At considerable cost we provided unleavened bread, as well as meat and wine—all strictly "Kosher." As we were nearly 2,000 strong at this time, the catering for the feast had to be most carefully gone into, and Lieut. Jabotinsky, Lieut. Lazarus, and the Rev. L. A. Falk did yeoman service in providing for all needs. It was a wonderful sight when we all sat down together and sang the Hagadah on the edge of the Sinai desert.

The Zionist Commission and Miss Berger, an American Zionist, helped us materially with funds, and our friends in England did likewise. The Acting Chairman of the Zionist Commission sent me the following letter for the occasion:—

Zionist Commission to Palestine,
c/o Chief Political Officer,
G.H.Q., Palestine.

Jerusalem, April 6, 1919.

To the Colonel of the 38th Battalion,
Col. J. H. Patterson, D.S.O.

My dear Colonel,

May I request, in the name of the Zionist Commission, that you have this letter read to the men of your battalion at their Seder Service.

The Commission is glad to be the means of aiding them in celebrating our Pesach, the Feast of Deliverance, and we trust that it will bring them all great joy. We have hopes now that our age-long prayers will soon be realized, and it should be a source of pride and happiness to them to know that they have contributed by their courage and their sacrifices toward its fulfilment. The Commission speaks in the name of the Zionist Organization in expressing to them the thanks of the nation for the devoted services they have rendered and are rendering, in the service of the liberty-loving nation, Great Britain, to which they have sworn fidelity, and to our people of Israel for whose future glory they have been willing to sacrifice their lives. The splendid part they have played, and will continue to play, will ever be remembered as a bright spot in the long history of our ancient people.

Very cordially yours,
(Signed) Harry Friedenwald,
Acting Chairman, Zionist Commission.

As Rafa was just over the border of Palestine, and therefore in the "Galuth," the Feast had to be kept for eight days. Many of the men thought that, as we were only a matter of yards from the boundary, I would on the eighth day issue leavened bread, which some of them were already hankering after, but this I would not hear of, and from that day forth I was considered the strictest Jew in the battalion!

CHAPTER XXVI

THE GREAT BOXING COMPETITION

There was a great deal of unrest and unhealthy excitement during demobilization, so to keep the troops interested and amused, competitions were got up throughout the E.E.F. in Boxing, Football, Cricket, and sports of all kinds.

Soon after we reached Rafa a programme of coming sporting events was circulated from G.H.Q.

Naturally, in a fighting army like the British, the greatest interest of all was taken in the Boxing competition, and the 38th Royal Fusiliers entered with keenness for all events.

By the terms of the contest teams could be chosen from Brigades, or even from Divisions, but, as we belonged to no Brigade or Division, we could only choose our men from our own battalion, which was of course a considerable handicap.

However, I considered that this was a grand opportunity of proving that men picked from this Jewish Battalion, if properly trained, would be able to hold their own against any team that might be brought against them from other units, or brigades, or even divisions, of the British Army.

I therefore formed a Sports Committee, collected my team of boxers, bought them boxing gloves, punch balls, etc., and despatched them with a trainer to El Arish, some 30 miles away, on the shores of the Mediterranean. There they raced, chased, boxed, bathed, danced, and were generally licked into condition by Sergeant Goldberg, the boxing instructor to the battalion.

In order to weed out the weaker teams so that only the very best should appear at the finals in Cairo, the contest was subdivided into four great tournaments: one for all the troops in Egypt, another for all the troops in Palestine, the third for all the troops in Syria, and the fourth for the best team among the Australians and New Zealanders. At my inspection of the 38th team, just before the tournament, I was much impressed with our prospects of success, for the men boxed wonderfully well.

We were all agog with excitement, and I may say with hope, when the great day for the Palestine Championship arrived and our men stepped inside the ropes at Kantara, surrounded by thousands of onlookers.

There was some splendid fighting, but I cannot go into the

details of it here. It is sufficient to say that we defeated all comers, won five gold medals, and emerged as the Champions of Palestine, with the right, therefore, of representing it in the great Cairo tournament for the Championship of the E.E.F. Could anything be more fitting? Jewish soldiers as champions of Palestine.

It can be imagined what jubilation there was in camp when our team returned to Rafa, and the ringing cheers which roared out when, at one of our concerts, I presented the gold medals to the victors, whose names are as follows:—

Heavy-weight Private Burack.
Welter-weight Private Tankinoff.
Light-weight Private Cohen.
Feather-weight Private Franks.
Bantam-weight Private Goldfarb.

The first round of this essentially British form of sport had been fought and won by the despised Jewish Battalion!

There yet remained the great contest at Cairo, where we would have to meet the champions of Egypt, and of the Australian forces, and of Syria.

Real hard training was once more the order of the day at El Arish, and I can guarantee that no fitter men than ours stepped into the ring at Cairo on that glorious night of the 13th March, when the first rounds of the championship were fought in the presence of thousands of spectators from all parts.

Again the Jewish Battalion won practically every contest, defeating all its opponents among the British Regiments. Eventually, it was left in to fight out the final round of the Championship for the whole of the E.E.F. with the Australians, who on their side had defeated their opponents.

It was a memorable night (the Ides of March) when this final contest took place. Excitement and feeling ran very high round the ring, and there was some magnificent fighting on both sides. In the end it was found that the Jewish Battalion had tied for victory with the Australians.

A decision, however, was given against us, on the grounds that we had not entered an officer of the battalion in the team. As a matter of fact, I had entered an officer of the battalion with the teams, but the judge (who was a British General, not an Australian) said that my team officer was only "attached" to the 38th for duty, and therefore could not be claimed as belonging to the battalion. Of course practically every officer in the battalion was only "attached" for duty, but there—I suppose it really would not have been the

110

"right thing" for one Jewish Battalion to have defeated the whole of the Egyptian Expeditionary Force!

In football the men were almost equally good, and we were good runners-up for the Championship of Palestine.

In cricket also—that essentially English game—the battalion acquitted itself most creditably under Captain Pope's tuition, defeating all comers in the Bir Salem matches, with the exception of the Flying Corps; while our Americans were, of course, unrivalled at base ball, at which they were real experts. They often gave exhibitions of their skill, to the great delight of all those who had never before seen the game played.

Our Concert Party was also still well to the fore, and easily took first place in Palestine—its only possible rival being that of the 39th Battalion. I had only got to let it be known that Tchaikov—our first violinist—would give a performance to draw a crowd big enough to pack our concert tent four times over. In the end a covetous man succeeded in wheedling Tchaikov away from us. Colonel Storrs, the Governor of Jerusalem, begged him from me so persuasively that I could not refuse him, more especially as it was to Tchaikov's advantage to settle in the Holy City, where he took up the post of Director of the School of Music.

CHAPTER XXVII

BIR SALEM—AN EXCITING RACE

Early in May we were transferred from Rafa to Bir Salem. The advance party moved on the 6th, and on the 10th the Battalion Headquarters followed, and took over duties from the 7th Indian Infantry Brigade, which was then sent to Haifa.

We were replaced at Rafa by the 40th (Jewish) Battalion Royal Fusiliers, which was now composed mainly of the Palestinian youths recruited by Major James de Rothschild and Lieutenant Lipsey. For a time they were commanded by Lieut.-Colonel F. D. Samuel D.S.O., but he left for England while the battalion was doing garrison duty at Haifa.

The command then fell to Colonel Scott, a most conscientious

111

officer, and a man in full sympathy with Zionist aspirations. While at Rafa he had a most anxious time owing to the unwise action of the military authorities. The men of the 40th Battalion had enlisted for service in Palestine only, but the local Staff ignored this definite contract and ordered part of the battalion to Cyprus. As this was a breach of their terms of enlistment, the men refused to go, and in the end the officials had to climb down and cancel all their unjust orders. Why did the Staff, when they knew all about this special contract for service in Palestine only, drive this excellent battalion almost to the verge of mutiny? There were many other battalions available for Cyprus.

Happily, Colonel Scott brought his men safely through the rough time at Rafa, and he served on with them until December, 1919, when the 40th was merged in the 38th Battalion.

All through the early days of May I saw chalked up everywhere—on the Railway Station, signal boxes, workshops, on the engines, trucks, and carriages—the mystic words, "Remember the 11th May."

This was, of course, the date on which all soldiers, rightly or wrongly, believed themselves entitled to their release, because it was six months after the Armistice granted to the Germans on November 11th, 1918.

I heard it rumoured that there was a conspiracy on foot in the E.E.F. for a general mutiny on that day, and found that men from other units had endeavoured to seduce my battalion from its duty.

On learning this, I at once determined to nip the attempt in the bud, and so made it my business to speak to every man in the battalion, and on every isolated post, impressing upon them the responsibility which rested on their shoulders as Jews, and urging them on no account to be led away by the hot-heads in other units.

I told them that British troops could perhaps afford to mutiny, but Jewish troops, while serving England, never.

I am proud to be able to state that not a man of my battalion failed on the 11th May, but just "carried on" as usual. Mutinies took place elsewhere, and thousands of British soldiers at Kantara ran riot and had the place in a blaze. However, the matter was hushed up, concessions were made, the mutineers were not punished, so far as I know, and things gradually became normal again.

Our effective strength when we left Rafa was 15 officers and 1,300 other ranks. Our duties at Bir Salem, Ludd, and Ramleh were exceptionally heavy, the men being very often on duty three nights in a week, and when they were off guard duties they were immediately put on to prisoner of war escorts, etc., as there was a very large Turkish and German Prisoners of War Camp at Ludd.

At Bir Salem we were attached to the 3rd (Lahore) Division, under the command of General Hoskin. It is a great pleasure to me to be able to state here that this officer and his Staff gave us a very hearty and cordial welcome to Bir Salem, and did everything possible for our comfort and welfare.

I look upon General Hoskin with his Staff as the one bright luminary amidst the gloomy British constellations among whom we were continually revolving! What an immense difference it makes to the feelings of a regiment or a battalion when it is known that the Staff are out to help and assist (as is their proper function), instead of to crab and block everything; in the former case one is ready to work the skin off one's bones, while in the latter everybody's back is up, with the result that co-ordination and happy working is impossible.

This was a happy time for the young lions of Judah, for the G.O.C. and his staff were out to help and assist in every possible way. We were not then aware of all the trials and tribulations that awaited us on the departure of General Hoskins and his excellent staff—sahibs to a man.

The battalion owes a deep debt of gratitude to Mr. Jessop, the capable secretary of the Y.M.C.A. in Egypt, who supplied us with a magnificent marquee, completely furnished with tables, chairs, forms, lamps, etc., etc. Only for this gift from the Y.M.C.A. we should have been very badly off indeed, for we were camped on a sandy waste without huts or any conveniences which other troops in our neighbourhood fortunately possessed.

It is a fact worthy of note that, although the wealthy Jews of Cairo and Alexandria contributed generously to the E. E. F. Comforts Fund, not a single article of any kind was ever sent to the Jewish Battalion to cheer them in their desolate surroundings. We asked for gramophones, etc., but got nothing—not even a reply!

There were compensations, however, at Bir Salem. We had many interesting visitors who came to cheer us in our camp in the sands, among others the Haham Bashi (Grand Rabbi of Jaffa) and the famous Dutch poet Dr. de Haan. I remember that the latter took great interest in a pet monkey which belonged to one of the men of the battalion, but the quaint-looking little animal showed little respect for the poet, for she evinced a decided desire to leave the print of her teeth in his finger as a souvenir of his visit.

We were always kindly and hospitably received by the citizens of Jaffa, headed by Mr. Bezalel Jaffe, and by those of Richon-le-Zion, headed by Mr. Gluskin, when we visited those colonies.

While stationed here I spent many a pleasant evening chatting with Mr. Aharoni, a well-known naturalist, who lives at Rechoboth.

113

There is perhaps no man in all Syria and Palestine with such a wide knowledge of the flora and fauna of those countries, and he gave me many interesting accounts of his adventures among the Bedouins while in quest of specimens for various European museums.

When the Great War broke out he had secured two live ostrich chicks, new to science, and these he had hoped to send alive to England. However, when the pinch for food came there was none for the ostriches, so they had to be killed; they were stuffed, and may now be seen at Lord Rothschild's famous museum at Tring Park, Hertfordshire. This story of the ostrich chicks was related to me by Mr. Aharoni while I was celebrating with him the "Feast of Tabernacles," under the shade of "boughs of goodly trees, branches of palm trees, and the boughs of thick trees, and willows of the brook," and we did greatly rejoice, for the Feast was a goodly one, and the pottage of Gevereth Aharoni was such as my soul loved.

About this time many military Race Meetings were organized in different parts of Palestine, Syria, and Egypt, and officers were encouraged to take part in them and get the men interested in the sport, so as to take their thoughts away from the absorbing topic of demobilization.

On the 5th June a Race Meeting was held at Surafend, a few miles from Bir Salem, and as we were all expected to support the programme, I entered my charger Betty for one of the events.

Betty was a beautiful dark-brown creature, but somewhat skittish and wayward, like many of her sex. I knew her little ways and how to humour her to perfection, and she always gave me of her best. More than once she managed to slip her fastenings in the horse lines, and used her freedom to gallop off to my tent, where she would thrust her head through the doorway; then, apparently satisfied, she would fly back to her place in the lines.

She appeared at times to see something not visible to the human eye, because, now and again, when cantering quickly along, for no apparent reason she would suddenly bound aside as if the Devil himself had scared her out of her wits.

The 3rd Lahore Division had at this time on its Staff an able and energetic sportsman, Major Pott, of the Indian Cavalry; this officer provided an excellent programme and ran the meeting without a hitch.

It was a lovely sunny afternoon, and thousands of people flocked to the course, soldiers from the camps round about, civilians from Jerusalem, Jaffa, and the surrounding colonies; the Arabs and Bedouins also sent a very strong contingent.

In the race for which I had entered Betty (I called her Betty in

114

memory of another Betty, also beautiful and with a turn of speed!) a full score of horses went to the post, and I, unfortunately, drew the outside place. I therefore felt that unless I got well away at the start, and secured sufficient lead to enable me to cross to the inside, I would have but a poor chance of winning, for, about half-way down the course, there was a tremendous bend to negotiate. I was lucky enough to jump away in front, and, soon finding myself well ahead, swerved across to the inside, where I hugged the rails. For three parts of the way round Betty made the running, but soon after we came into the straight for home I eased her a bit and was passed by Major Pott, who was riding a well-known mare, also, strange to say, called Betty. At the distance the Major was quite a length ahead of me, but I felt that there was still plenty of go in my Betty, so I called upon the game little mare to show her mettle. Gradually she forged herself forward until there was but a head between them, and for the last dozen strides the two Bettys raced forward dead level amid the frantic roars of the crowd, all shouting, "Go on, Betty! Go on, Betty!" We both rode for all we were worth, my Betty straining every nerve to defeat her namesake, and finally, amid terrific cheering, by the shortest of heads, Betty won—but, alas, it was the other Betty!

CHAPTER XXVIII

DAMASCUS

Towards the end of June I took part in the military races at Alexandria, and from the "home town" of Hypatia I took ship and went to Beyrout—a lovely seaport, nestling under the mighty and magnificent Lebanon. Here I was most hospitably entertained by my friends, the Bustroses. From the balcony of her palatial residence Madame Bustros enjoys a view second to none in the world, and every imaginable fruit and flower grows and blooms on her estate. Beyrout is undoubtedly a place of milk and honey, and is unquestionably within the Biblical boundaries of the Promised Land. Ezekiel xlvii., 17, states: "and the border from the sea shall be Hazar-enan, the border of Damascus and the north northward and the border of Hamath." This was the northern boundary assigned to Israel and was actually occupied in the days of David and Solomon.

My journey across the Lebanon was one long feast of the most beautiful scenery in the world. As we topped the range my last peep of mountain and valley, stretching away down to Beyrout, hemmed in by the glittering sea, was like a vision of Paradise.

Instead of going to Damascus direct, I branched off at Ryak and ran up the Bakaa, the valley which stretches between Lebanon and Anti-Lebanon to Baalbek, where I spent a wonderful time amid the mighty ruins of that ancient temple to Baal.

Baalbek is the most beautiful and impressive ruin that it has ever been my good fortune to look upon. Thebes may exceed it in size, but the wonder of Egypt had not the effect upon me that was produced when I stood under the magnificent columns of this great temple to the heathen god.

I wandered through the vast pile, an insignificant speck amidst its gigantic pillars and fallen lintels, overthrown and shattered by the devastating earthquake which centuries ago wrecked this mighty structure. Who were the architects who designed it? and who were the engineers who set on high those stupendous blocks? Verily there were giants in those days.

At Baalbek railway station I came across one of the prettiest girls I had seen for many a long day engaged in selling peaches. She was a Syrian from Lebanon, which is noted for the beauty of its maidens; I overheard her companions address this Houri of the mountains as "Edeen." While I was standing waiting for my train to arrive a dust storm suddenly sprang up, and when it was over Edeen sat down and calmly licked the dust off every peach until they all bloomed again in her basket; then presently she presented the fruit, fresh and shining, to the incoming passengers, who eagerly bought it from the smiling damsel! I need hardly say that peaches were "off" for me during the rest of my trip, for not all sellers were as beautiful as Edeen!

A few hours in the train took me over the Anti-Lebanon, and I caught my first glimpse of Damascus, that most ancient of cities, which I had long desired to see.

When Mohammed was a camel driver, making a caravan journey from Medina to Aleppo, the story goes that he once camped on a hill overlooking Damascus. His companions asked him to join them and go into the city but he replied—"No; Paradise should only be entered after death!"

I viewed the city from the same spot, but, not being so sure of my hereafter as was the Prophet, I decided to take my chance of entering this earthly Paradise while it offered.

116

It is rightly described as a pearl set in emeralds. White mosques, minarets, and cupolas peep dazzlingly in all directions out of the emerald foliage. Trees, gardens, and flowers of all kinds abound in this delectable city, whose charm is enhanced by the murmur of the many rivers running through it. I, too, like Naaman the Syrian, found "Abana and Pharpar, rivers of Damascus, better than all the waters of Israel." The latter is in the district, and runs some ten miles to the south of the oldest city in the world. The great Saladin is buried in Damascus, and of course I made a pilgrimage to the tomb of this famous warrior.

I like to avoid the caravanserais set up for Europeans as much as possible when travelling in the East, so that I may see something of the life of the people. In this way one has many pleasant little adventures, experiences and remembrances, which give zest to life.

While lunching at a famous Arab restaurant I made the acquaintance of Dr. Yuseff, a well-known medical man of Damascus and Beyrout; among other subjects we talked horses and races, and we became such good friends that he lent me his fiery, pure-bred Arab steed to ride while sight-seeing in the neighbourhood—a sure token of friendship from this cultured Arab of Syria.

Just on the outskirts of the city on the banks of the river Barada (the Biblical Abana) I had noticed a Bedouin camp crowded with good-looking horses, so thither I went and called on the Sheik of the tribe. While sitting with the elders in a huge circle, sipping coffee out of tiny cups, I discovered from their conversation that my hosts were wandering Kurds, who were just about to set off for the confines of Persia. I hinted that I would like to join their caravan, and was immediately given a warm welcome, but, much as I should have liked to roam the desert with them, I had to think of my Jewish Battalion waiting for me at Bir Salem. The Kurds expressed much interest when I told them I had to go on a pilgrimage to El Kuds (meaning Jerusalem), for of course they were good Moslems and reverenced the Holy City.

On leaving Damascus I travelled down the Hedjaz Railway as far as Deraa. The moment the ancient Syrian capital is left the train enters the desert, the home of the Ishmaelite. These bold rovers, from time immemorial, have hunted and harried the peaceful traveller caught toiling through their fastnesses. We were not molested for the simple reason that troops of cavalry, British and Indian, were posted at strategic points all along the railway. A few months later, when we withdrew from these parts, the Bedouins began their old games, and took a fierce joy in derailing trains, and robbing, and even killing, the passengers. In this way a good friend of mine, Comandante Bianchini, an officer of the Royal Italian

Navy, met his untimely end at the hands of these desert marauders. Bianchini was deeply interested in, and worked hard for, the Zionist cause, and his loss is a sad blow to his many friends. A more cheery, lovable man never sailed the seas.

We reached Deraa (the ancient Edrei) without incident, and then branched off westward to Haifa, the train clambering down and around the precipitous sides of the Yarmuk Escarpment, past the southern shore of the Lake of Galilee at Samakh, across the Jordan and running parallel to it for some miles, then curving upwards out of the Jordan Valley, into the valley of Jezreel, which continues into the plain of Esdraelon.

These narrow plains, the heritage of Issachar, sever the head of Palestine from the body, or, in other words, separate Galilee from Samaria and Judæa. To use an Irishism, this neck had been the "Achilles' heel" of Israel throughout her history. All down the ages armies from Babylonia, Assyria, Persia, and Egypt have marched and counter-marched through this fertile belt. Open passes southward made Samaria an easy prey. Beisan (the ancient Bethshan), which guards the eastern end and dominates the passage over the Jordan, was generally in the hands of the stranger. It was in the neighbourhood of this famous old stronghold that Barak defeated Sisera, captain of the host of Jaban, king of the Canaanites—a victory celebrated in the famous song of Deborah. It was also in this neighbourhood that Gideon smote the Midianites. His motto, "The sword of the Lord and of Gideon," was also the motto of the Zionists who served England so stoutly in Gallipoli, and it was a curious coincidence that, just as the Midianites were routed by the shouting and clamour of Gideon's three companies, so was the Turkish Army routed by the Zion mules when, with rattling chains and clattering hoofs, they stampeded one dark night and galloped through the Turks as they were creeping stealthily up to attack the British trenches.

Later on in the military history of the Israelites we find the Philistines battling for the supremacy on these plains and overthrowing the army of Israel under their first King Saul, who, in the bitterness of defeat, and finding he could not escape, fell on his sword and died on Mount Gilboa. In the same battle and the same place the death of Jonathan put an end to his immortal friendship with David and called forth the famous lament: "The beauty of Israel is slain upon thy high places; how are the mighty fallen."

These stories of the Old Testament flashed vividly through my mind as we rolled onward through this historic valley between Mount Gilboa and Beisan on the left, and the cone-shaped Mount Tabor away on the right.

Other countries and other scenes were recalled to my mind when I spied half a dozen beautiful antelope near some standing corn, and my thoughts of Africa were further intensified when I caught a glimpse, on the railway bank, of a huge black snake, some six feet long, rapidly darting away out of danger.

Soon afterwards, on looking to the north, I saw Nazareth perched upon a southern Galilean hill-top. We wound in and out by the brook Kishon, where Elijah smote the false prophets. Finally we passed along the mighty shoulder of Mount Carmel into that great natural anchorage of Haifa, nestling under its shadow; then southward to Ludd and Bir Salem—the whole train journey from Damascus taking some fifteen hours and giving me an unrivalled feast of Biblical landscapes.

Early in July I visited Acre to take part in the races there (which proved a fiasco owing to the antics of the starter), and suddenly found myself close to the dwelling of the famous Abdul Baha, the exponent of the doctrine of the Brotherhood of Man. He certainly has a wide field before him, for at the present moment there seems to be very little brotherly love in any part of the world! His particular mission is to unite the peoples of the earth, and do away with all barriers of race, creed, and prejudice.

Since Patriarchs, Popes, Archbishops, Mullahs, and ministers of all creeds have failed to make humanity realise the necessity of "brotherly love," the League of Nations would be well advised to adopt the Sage of Acre and make him President of a "League of Teachers," pledged to inculcate love for one's fellowmen as the cardinal feature of his curriculum. One thing is certain—the League of Nations will never bring the world into harmony unless the young are taught to love and help their brothers, irrespective of nationality.

It will be remembered that Acre was the town to which Napoleon laid siege after his wonderful march from Egypt with about 10,000 French Infantry. This extraordinary man was able to cross the Sinai desert with his army, without either roads, railway, or water supply, capture Gaza, Jaffa, and Haifa with ease, and only for the British Fleet would undoubtedly have added Acre, and probably all Syria, to his spoils.

Those who have traversed the Sinai sands in a comfortable railway coach can afford to pay a warm tribute to this redoubtable warrior, and to the no less redoubtable Infantry of France.

119

CHAPTER XXIX

AMONG THE PHILISTINES

When General Hoskin left Bir Salem to take up a command in England he was replaced by Major-General Sir John Shea, under whom we had served for a short time in the line. If this officer had not been called elsewhere, I am quite sure that the regrettable incidents which I shall have to relate would never have taken place; but, unfortunately, General Shea was away practically all the time we were attached to his Division, and a senior Brigadier acted in his place.

This Brigadier was apparently well aware of the anti-Jewish attitude taken up by certain members of the G.H.Q. Staff, and trimmed his sails accordingly, but unfortunately for himself, as the sequel will show, his zeal to second their ill-advised efforts carried him to such lengths that even those influential members whose policy he was supporting were unable to save him from the consequences of his own outrageous folly.

No sooner had we come under his command than his anti-Semitic bias became apparent. Certain areas were placed out of bounds to "Jewish soldiers" but not to men in other battalions. Jewish soldiers were so molested by the Military Police that the only way they could enjoy a peaceful walk outside camp limits was by removing their Fusilier badges and substituting others which they kept conveniently in their pockets for the purpose. They found that by adopting this method they were never interfered with by the Military Police.

Traditional British fair play seemed to have taken wings as soon as General Z. appeared on the scene. I repeatedly made official complaints about the way the men were persecuted, but nothing was done to mend matters. As a British officer I felt ashamed to hold my head up in my own camp owing to the unfair and un-English treatment to which the men were subjected.

It may well be imagined that this attitude of the Staff made my command anything but an easy one. In the first place, knowing how all ranks were discriminated against, no officer or man wished to remain in the battalion. It was exceedingly difficult under the circumstances to get the best out of the men. While we were with the Anzacs, although we suffered exceedingly from the deadly climate in the desolate Jordan Valley, yet we were all thoroughly

120

happy, because we were treated with justice and sympathy by the Staff and by all other ranks in that famous division. At Bir Salem, on the contrary, we were anything but a happy unit.

It will be remembered that before we left Rafa the battalion had been swamped by about 800 recruits. Physically they were a very fine lot, but, being young and hailing from the United States, they were a bit wild and difficult to handle. The moment they joined the battalion they had to do real hard soldiering, and were put on outposts and detachments up and down the country, guarding thousands of prisoners of war, long stretches of railway line, millions of pounds worth of munitions, food, ordnance supplies, etc. In fact, so arduous were these duties that the men had scarcely more than every alternate night in bed, although it is the rule in the army that whenever possible every man should be allowed at least three consecutive nights' rest.

The great majority of my old trained men of the 38th had by this time either been demobilised, invalided to England, or employed on special duties between Cairo and Aleppo, so that a great part of the heavy duties which had to be carried out fell on the American recruits. There was absolutely no time to train these men, and I consider it was really wonderful that they did so well under the circumstances.

I know of no more heart-breaking task for a Commanding Officer than to endeavour to keep a battalion in a high state of discipline when he is surrounded by a hostile staff, apparently all out to irritate and humiliate both officers and men. From "reveille" to "lights out" it was a case of countering the actions of those in authority which constantly tended to create discontent and ill-feeling in our ranks.

I may mention that I had scores of protests from the men, often daily, owing to the persecution to which they were subjected while we were at Bir Salem. Is it to be wondered at that, suffering all these things, some of the American volunteers at last became restive and asked themselves, "Why should we serve England and be treated like dogs?"

I often felt it necessary to speak to the men, for I knew that their loyalty was strained almost to breaking-point. At such moments I told them that the honour of Jewry rested on their shoulders, and no matter what provocation they might be subjected to, they must at all times remain steadfast. The Imperial Government in England was sound and sympathetic to their ideals, and eventually justice must prevail, and the evil days through which we were passing would soon come to an end. I appealed to them as

Jews to be good soldiers, and, to their credit, they always responded.

Before this persecution became acute volunteers were called for to serve with the Army of Occupation in Palestine. Several hundred American enthusiasts in the battalion offered their services, but owing to the treatment they received their enthusiasm died out, and they requested that they should be demobilized and repatriated. A small party of these American citizens who were on outpost duty at Belah, some sixty miles to the south of Bir Salem, sent in a signed memorial requesting demobilization; otherwise they stated that they would refuse to do duty after a certain date which was mentioned. This document I, of course, forwarded to Divisional Headquarters.

I had been writing to the authorities for months, requesting that these men should be demobilized and sent back to the United States, and at last I heard, unofficially, that the order for repatriation was on its way.

I sent my adjutant to inform the Belah men that their release was coming through in the course of a few days, and to tell them to carry on meanwhile like good soldiers.

More than half of the men responded, but the rest, being young and untrained, refused to perform any further soldierly duties after the expiry of the time limit; they just remained quietly in their tents, for they wished to bring matters to a head.

I am glad to say that the Jewish soldiers, both Americans and British, serving with me at Bir Salem, stood firm and carried out their duties as usual.

After personal investigation into the conduct of these foolish youths at Belah I remanded them for trial by Field General Court Martial, and forwarded the charge sheets, with summaries of evidence, to General Z. I had framed the charge sheets most carefully, but apparently my drafting did not suit the General, for he framed fresh charges of mutiny, and sent his A.D.C. with them to me for immediate signature. I had but a moment to scan the charge sheets, for the A.D.C. was impatient to catch a train which was due to leave. I did not like the General's drafting, but, being a very obedient soldier, I duly signed the documents as ordered and handed them back to the waiting Staff officer, wishing him luck with them as he galloped off.

According to King's Regulations, a soldier remanded for trial by Court Martial has the right to request the help of an officer to act as his friend at the trial, and, of course, it is the bounden duty of such officer to do everything in his power to get the accused acquitted. The Belah men petitioned Lieutenant Jabotinsky to act as

122

their advocate, and he, somewhat unwillingly, assented to undertake the ungrateful task. He was not anxious to defend these men of Belah because he held that they should have carried out their duties faithfully to the end, even although they felt that they had a grievance against authority.

The trial took place at Kantara, and, in the course of it, Lieutenant Jabotinsky pointed out a fatal flaw in the charge sheets, with the result that the charge of mutiny failed, and the Court had to be dissolved. The President (who belonged to Major-General Louis Jean Bols' late Regiment) was furious at the fiasco, and said, "This is all the fault of Colonel Patterson, and I shall report him." My adjutant, Captain Sandison, a staunch and sturdy Scot, was present in Court as Prosecutor, and, knowing all the facts of the case, at once turned on the President and said, "You have no right, Sir, to make such a statement about my Commanding Officer. The G.O.C. Division rejected his charge sheets, which were in perfect order, and framed the faulty ones himself, so now you know whom to report."

A new Court had to be convened, but the men were now arraigned merely on the lesser charge of disobeying an order. Even on this lesser charge they were savagely sentenced to various terms of penal servitude, ranging from seven years downwards. Had they been found guilty by the first Court on the charge of mutiny I presume they would all have been shot!

I am confident that if these young Americans had been properly trained as soldiers, this Belah incident would never have taken place. I had given the authorities ample warning of what was likely to happen when these recruits were thrust upon me, but my advice was ignored.

All I can say is that if an Australian, English, Irish, or a Scottish battalion had been treated as this Jewish battalion was treated, Divisional Headquarters would have gone up in flames and the General himself would have been lucky to escape.

Be it noted that the mutineers of other British units, the men who had openly defied all authority and set Kantara in a blaze, were not even put on trial!

Until the recruits were forcibly thrust upon me, I can vouch for it that the 38th Battalion Royal Fusiliers was one of the most exemplary units that ever took the field, crime being practically unknown. The men endured hard marching, hard knocks, fatiguing manual labour, at times scanty rations of food and water, the seething heat of the Jordan Valley and the anti-Semitism of the local military authorities, and withal gained the highest praise from the General Officer Commanding under whom they served in the field.

Notwithstanding the fact that we were so despitefully used, the authorities found that the men's services were invaluable. In addition to garrisoning large areas of Palestine, I had officers, N.C.O.s, and men, holding all kinds of important posts throughout the E.E.F., from Aleppo to Cairo. The demand for men from the 38th Battalion was ever on the increase, for executive officers found the Jewish soldier steady, sober and reliable, three qualities, the importance of which I was always impressing on the men, although, as a matter of fact, sobriety is one of the outstanding virtues of the Jewish soldier.

CHAPTER XXX

THE FALL OF GOLIATH

The violent anti-Semitism shown by General Z at last reached such a pitch that on one occasion (the 16th July to be exact), he rode into camp and, without the slightest provocation, abused and insulted the men, threatened one of them, and actually went so far as to strike an unoffending private soldier with his whip, using at the same time language which would make Billingsgate blush.

I was not present at this outrage, but I heard a full account of all that happened from various eye-witnesses who reported the affair, and all I could imagine was that the General must have suddenly gone insane.

The whole battalion was in an uproar, and I had much ado to pacify the men and keep things going.

The man who was struck was sent to Hospital with a swollen arm, and the other men who were specifically insulted reported to me at the orderly room and complained of the treatment they had received. I forwarded their complaint to General Z, together with the sick report of the man he had struck with his whip. He replied requesting me to have these particular men paraded so that he might speak to them.

I arranged for this embarrassing interview, and, to prevent any hostility which the outraged battalion might have shown towards General Z when he entered the camp, I kept the men in their tents, with N.C.O.s in charge of each door, with instructions to see that no untoward incident took place.

On arrival the General apologised to the insulted men, but so indignant were they that at first they refused to accept it, or to shake hands when he offered to do so. Finally, after over half-an-hour's persuasion, they agreed to accept his apology, provided it was given publicity, and also to the whole battalion on parade. This he did very fully, and I sincerely hoped that the incident was happily ended, and that for the future, in dealing with us, General Z would see that no injustice was done merely because we were Jews.

To compensate for all the misfortunes we were called upon to endure, our life in the battalion itself was quite smooth and happy, all pulling well together.

Personally, I took no thought whether a man was a Jew or a Gentile; I remember that an officer joined us while we were serving at the front, and, through some misunderstanding, I took him to be a Jewish officer. He distinguished himself later and earned the M.C., which pleased me very much, for I was always glad when I was able to recommend a Jewish officer for promotion or reward. I sent this officer with nine others to form a "Minyan" (the number required to hold a Jewish religious service) at the burial of a Jewish soldier who was killed on the day we captured the Umm esh Shert Ford, and it was not until after this incident happened that I discovered he was a Gentile.

There was one exception, however, to the general harmony and esprit de corps of the battalion. A Staff officer was sent to do duty with us from G.H.Q., where he had been employed for over a year. Some time after his arrival he publicly insulted one of my Jewish officers and refused to apologise. The matter was then brought before me, and, as he still remained obdurate, I brought him before General Z. When asked by the latter why he had insulted the Jewish officer his reply was, "I don't like Jews. The Jews are not liked at G.H.Q., and you know it, Sir." The General ordered him to apologise, which I must say he did most handsomely, but his remarks about the dislike of Jews at G.H.Q., though no news to me or the General, may be somewhat illuminating to the reader!

Although we hoped that all unpleasantness with the General was over, I regret to say that this was not the case. I could give many instances of unfair treatment to which we were subjected, but I will not weary the reader by relating them here. After his apology the General never again came near us, and every indignity, slight and petty tyranny that could be invented was put upon the battalion. The whole subsequent attitude of the G.O.C. showed us that his apology was merely eye-wash, and had simply been extracted from him by fear of the consequences of his outrageous behaviour.

In fact, in the end, I had to bring his conduct to the notice of the Commander-in-Chief, with the result that he was removed from his Command and no longer troubled Israel.

CHAPTER XXXI

PROTESTS

In case any readers may think that my account is exaggerated I give some letters of protest which I received from some of the officers in my battalion. From this it will be seen what a difficult position I was placed in, owing to the policy of G.H.Q. towards Jewish aspirations.

A few interested parties, for their own ends, sedulously spread the rumour that there was no anti-Semitism shown in Palestine. I will leave the reader to judge whether these people were knaves or fools:

LUDD,
4-7-19,
A7/48.

SIR,

I beg to report that the men are discontented, not only in our battalion, but also in the other Jewish units, which cannot fail to influence our men still more.

The causes of their discontent are much deeper than delay of Demobilization. Over 3/7ths of the Judæans in this country are men who volunteered to serve in Palestine in the name of their Zionist ideals, and in reply to the pledge embodied in the declaration which Mr. Balfour, on behalf of H.M. Government, issued on the 2nd November, 1917.

It is now a general impression among our soldiers, an impression shared by the public opinion of Palestine, that this pledge has been broken, so far as local authorities are concerned.

Palestine has become the theatre of an undisguised anti-Semitic policy. Elementary equality of rights is denied the Jewish

126

inhabitants; the Holy City, where the Jews are by far the largest community, has been handed over to a militantly anti-Semitic municipality; violence against Jews is tolerated, and whole districts are closed to them by threats of such violence under the very eyes of the authorities; high officials, guilty of acts which any Court would qualify as instigation to anti-Jewish pogroms, not only go unpunished, but retain their official positions. The Hebrew language is officially disregarded and humiliated; anti-Semitism and anti-Zionism is the fashionable attitude among officials who take their cue from superior authority; and honest attempts to come to an agreement with Arabs are being frustrated by such means as penalising those Arab notables who betray pro-Jewish feeling.

The Jewish soldier is treated as an outcast. The hard and honest work of our battalions is recompensed by scorn and slander, which, starting from centres of high authority, have now reached the rank and file, and envenomed the relations between Jewish and English soldiers. When there is a danger of anti-Jewish excesses, Jewish soldiers are removed from the threatened areas and employed on fatigues, and not even granted the right to defend their own flesh and blood.

Passover was selected to insult their deepest religious feelings, by barring them access to the Wailing Wall during that week. No Jewish detachment is allowed to be stationed in Jerusalem or any of the other Holy Cities of Jewry.

When a Jewish sentry is attacked and beaten by a dozen drunken soldiers, and a drunken officer disarms with ignominy a Jewish guard, nobody is punished. Leave to certain towns has become a torture because the Military Police have been specially instructed to hunt the Jew, and the weaker ones among our men escape this humiliation by concealing their regimental badge, and substituting the badge of some other unit.

In addition, army pledges given to them are also disregarded; men who were recruited for service in Palestine are sent against their will to Messina or Egypt or Cyprus; men who enlisted under the understanding that their pay would be equal to that of any British soldier suddenly discover that no allowances will be paid to their wives and children.

Under these conditions, even some of the best among them give way to despair; they see no purpose in carrying on, conscious that the great pledge has been broken, that instead of a National Home for the Jewish people, Palestine has become the field of operations of official anti-Semitism; they abhor the idea of

127

*covering with their tacit connivance what they—and not they
alone—consider a fraud.*

*They cannot formulate these grievances in full, nor gather
the documents necessary to prove them, but under their desire to
"get out of the show" there is bitter disappointment, one of the most
cruel even in Jewish history.*

*You, Sir, have always been in favour of speeding up their
demobilization; I, as you know, was of the opinion that it is the
duty of every volunteer to stick to the Jewish Regiment as long as
circumstances might demand, and I still hope that many will stick
to it in spite of all. But even I myself am compelled to admit that
things have reached a stage when no further moral sacrifice can
fairly be demanded of men whose faith has been shattered.*

*I only hope that those who give up the struggle will not
follow the example of a few misguided irresponsibles who chose
the wrong way to support a right claim. I hope that they will await
their release in a calm and dignified manner, discharging their
duties to the last moment, and thus giving those who misrule this
country a lesson in fair play—a lesson badly needed.*

I remain, Sir,
Your obedient Servant,
XX.

To Lieutenant-Colonel J. H. Patterson,
D.S.O., Commanding 38th Battalion
Royal Fusiliers.

Bir Salem,
17-7-1919.

To Officer Commanding
38th Royal Fusiliers.

Sir,

*I have the honour to request that this application praying
that I may be permitted to resign my Commission in His Majesty's
Forces be forwarded through the usual channels, together with the
undermentioned reasons for my taking this step after having
originally volunteered for the Army of Occupation.*

*My resignation, Sir, is my only method of protest against
the grossly unfair and all too prevalent discrimination against the
battalion to which I have the honour to belong. I desire to point out
to you, Sir, the fact that this unfair and un-British attitude affects
not only my honour as a Jew, but my prestige as a British officer,
and this latter point must inevitably handicap me in the efficient
discharge of my military duties.*

The disgraceful exhibition of yesterday morning is but a

fitting climax to the endless series of insults and annoyances to which this battalion—because it is a Jewish Battalion—has been subjected, almost since our first arrival in the E.E.F. Insults to a battalion as a whole, Sir, are insults directed to every individual member of that battalion, and as long as I remain a member of His Majesty's Forces, I regret to say I find myself unable to fittingly resent in a manner compatible with my own honour, and the honour of my race, the insulting attitude towards my race, and through my race, towards me, of my military superiors.

In passing, may I point out that my being a Jew did not prevent me doing my duty in France, in Flanders, and in Palestine, and in the name of the countless dead of my race who fell doing their duty in every theatre of war, I resent, and resent very strongly indeed, the abusive attitude at present prevalent towards Jewish troops.

I have innumerable instances of petty spite, and not a few cases of a very serious character indeed, all of which I can readily produce should the occasion ever arise.

I have the honour to be, Sir,
Your obedient Servant,
Y.Y.

It was not only my Jewish officers who found life unbearable under these conditions, but the other officers also felt the strain.

I received the following letter from one of my senior Christian Officers after an outburst on the part of the Staff:

To the O.C.
38th Battalion Royal Fusiliers.

Sir,

I have the honour to request that I be immediately relieved of my duties and permitted to proceed to England for demobilization. I am 40 years of age, and have had nothing except my desire to do my duty to keep me in the Service. The impossible conditions forced on the battalion by higher authority are too much for me, and I very much regret that I should have to trouble you with this application at the present time.

I have the honour to be, Sir,
Your obedient Servant,
SS.

Bir Salem,
24th August, 1919.

Letters such as these give some slight conception of the extremely difficult position in which I was placed. On the one hand I had to ward off the blows aimed at the battalion by the local military authorities, while on the other hand I had to do my utmost to allay the angry feelings of my officers, N.C.O.s, and men, goaded almost to desperation by the attitude adopted towards the battalion.

This anti-Jewish policy was directed not only against the Jewish Battalions, but also, in a flagrant manner, against the Jewish civil population, upon whom every indignity was poured; in fact, the British Military Administration made of the famous Balfour Declaration—the declared policy of the British Government—a byword and a laughing stock.

Early in 1919 the Chief Administrator then in office in Palestine, the man who represented the British Government, offered a public insult to the Jews at a Jewish Concert, by deliberately sitting down and ordering his staff to do the same when the Hatikvah, the Jewish national hymn, was being sung, while, of course, all others were standing. This was as deliberate an insult as could be offered to the feelings of any people. England must be in a bad way when a man such as this is appointed to represent her as Governor.

Judge Brandies, of the United States Supreme Court, visited Palestine about the time when these anti-Jewish manifestations were at their height, and was shocked and horrified at the un-English attitude he saw adopted towards the Jews and all things Jewish.

I myself told him of the mockery of the Balfour Declaration as exemplified by the British Military Administration in Palestine, and said I thought it was a pity that Mr. Balfour had not added three more words to his famous utterance. The Judge asked me what words I meant, and I said they were that Palestine was to be a national home for "the baiting of" the Jewish people!

I know that Judge Brandies went home hurriedly, very much perturbed at what he heard and saw, which was so contrary in everything to the spirit of the declared policy of England. He represented the state of affairs in Palestine to Downing Street, with the result that the local military authorities were told that the policy as laid down in the Balfour Declaration must be carried out.

This was a sad blow to those purblind ones who had looked forward to a long rule in the Middle East; for them the writing was already on the wall.

I want it to be clearly understood that this attitude was merely the policy of the local military officials who, by their attitude, were practically defying and deriding the policy of England, as expressed by the Home Government.

CHAPTER XXXII

A TRIP TO THE SEA OF GALILEE

I had long looked forward to a visit to the Sea of Galilee (Lake Tiberias), and eventually, late in October, my ambition was fulfilled, for, taking advantage of "Damascus week," when leave was easy to get, I slipped off from Ludd one morning at 8.30, and arrived at Samakh, on the southern shores of the sea, at 2 o'clock in the afternoon.

My first peep of the Lake, as it stretched out before me and melted away in the purple haze to the north, was delightful. The colouring was superb and, as I sat on the edge of the rickety pier, I drank in my novel surroundings with all the enthusiasms of a rapturous pilgrim.

The Lake glistened and glinted in the brilliant sunshine, the abrupt arid-looking hill-sides deepened the silent mystery that seemed to hang over it. Away to the right was the spot where the Gadarene swine, possessed of the evil spirit, rushed down to the sea and destroyed themselves.

Peering through my glasses straight north, I could see in the shimmering distance the dense groves of evergreens which told me that this was the place where the Jordan plunged down from "the waters of Merom" through a rocky gorge, and entered the Lake. Away to the left I caught a glimpse of a few trees and houses, and I realized that I was looking at Capernaum, the place in which it will be remembered the worthy Roman Centurion built a synagogue. Glancing further west, and somewhat nearer to me, I saw the site of Bethsaida; sweeping further westward and yet nearer, the round towers and rectangular walls of Tiberias itself stood revealed, while close to my left hand, at the south-west corner of the Lake, the thriving Jewish colony of Kinnereth overlooked the spot where the Jordan rushed out of the Lake on its way to the Dead Sea.

Round about me were children revelling in the limpid water, and even a few discreetly-veiled damsels displayed a fair share of their neat limbs, while paddling along the sandy shore in the shade of the cliffs.

Suddenly, into all this old-world scenery, there dashed a lively motor-boat, which had come from Tiberias to collect passengers. We scrambled down from the crazy pier, and within an hour found ourselves climbing up the rickety gangway leading to Tiberias, a city which stands to-day much as King Herod Antipas, the builder, left it, although, in the meantime, it has been much devastated by earthquakes.

I was agreeably surprised to find a clean and fairly comfortable hotel, most capably managed by Frau Grossmann. It was still hot at Tiberias, and yet, by some mysterious means, Frau Grossmann always managed to produce a bottle of cold beer for dinner, a most grateful drink in this thirsty valley.

In the early morning, I hired a boat with a good-humoured Arab crew of three, and made an expedition across to Capernaum. Fish are still as plentiful here as they were in the days of Simon Peter, and the Capernaum fishermen still cast their nets as they did in apostolic times, and wear just as little clothing.

As I wandered among the ruins, I met a striking Franciscan, Father Vendelene, who was hospitality itself. He was a venerable German, a very fine-looking man, standing over six feet high, full of Christian charity, and apparently resigned to the blow which had fallen upon his nation. Besides being a monk he was also an architect and had built many monasteries, convents, and churches for the Franciscans in many parts of the world; but he had been a soldier before he became a monk, and I noticed, as he smoked a pipe and related to me his varied career, that his eyes glowed, and his broad shoulders were thrown back, as he described how he charged at the head of his squadron of Hussars in one of the battles of the Franco-Prussian War. The good Father took me round what was left of the synagogue built by the worthy Centurion whose servant was healed. It must have been a fine piece of architecture in its day, and it is a thousand pities that it has been levelled to the ground by an earthquake.

On my return to the hotel I found that two Nursing Sisters had arrived from Egypt to spend a few days at Tiberias, and at dinner I suggested that they should join me in my boat on a voyage of discovery which I intended to make across the Lake on the following morning, and to this they readily agreed.

The Military Governor of Tiberias had very kindly arranged for a mounted escort and a horse to be ready for me at the north end of the Lake where the Jordan enters it, as I wished to make an exploring expedition as far as possible up the river towards Lake Merom.

We left Tiberias at dawn and had a most delightful trip across the Lake, breakfasting in the boat on the way. Sister Cook, who was blessed with a charming voice, was moved to song, and the time passed so pleasantly that before we knew where we were, we found ourselves stuck on a sandbar in the Jordan River itself. Our

132

boatmen hopped out, pushed the boat over the bar into deep water, and off we paddled again up the famous river. Great fields of ripe maize stretched away on either hand, and it was curious to see dusky youths perched aloft on stagings, armed with a sling, doing slaughter among any birds that dared to settle on their crops. We shoved the nose of our boat into the bank, took a stroll along a path through the tangled undergrowth, and soon met a crowd of Bedouins who presented us with some delicious maize cobs. In this manner we pleasantly meandered up the Jordan, now landing on this bank, and now on that, as it took our fancy, until at last a point was reached where the river was so shallow that the boat could go no further, and here I found my pony and escort awaiting me.

The latter was composed of local mounted Arab gendarmerie, under the command of a Jewish corporal, who had at one time served in the 40th Battalion Royal Fusiliers, and I noticed with pleasure that the Jew and the Arabs seemed to be on excellent terms.

I charged the boatman to take the Sisters to Capernaum, where I told them to call on Father Vendelene, who I knew would give them a warm welcome.

Having seen the boat safely started on the way, and with strict injunctions to the sailors to return for me in good time, I mounted my pony and started my exploration of the Upper Jordan.

My escort (who were also supposed to be guides) often got completely lost in the dense oleander jungle that here abounds, but after many trials and tribulations, in the course of which I came upon a submerged herd of buffalo sleeping peacefully in a marshy backwater, I emerged torn and bleeding at the entrance of the black rocky gorge down which the Jordan rushes. Riding here became impossible, so I went on foot until the westering sun warned me it was time to return.

On the way back, which was by another and much easier route, we came across a stalwart Bedouin hunter who, only five days before, had shot a splendid leopard on the hillside.

I asked him if there was any chance of my being able to do likewise. He replied that it was possible, but I might have to wait a month before I got a shot; I could, however, have other good hunting any day I liked, for the thickets were alive with wild boar. This man knew every track round about, and, as we were still shut in by dense thickets, he volunteered to come with me as a guide to the Lake. On parting he refused all offers of money, but later I sent him some tobacco, which I hope he received safely. My escort, when we reached open level country, raced and chased each other on their ponies, pulling up suddenly, or darting to the right or left in wild

133

career. Both rode thoroughbred Arab mares and were immensely proud of their steeds, and their own prowess thereon.

On reaching the Lake, I espied the boat coming along, and as the water was shallow I urged my mount into it and rode out to meet the little vessel. The Arab boatmen, singing some quaint chorus, came alongside and I slipped off the saddle on to the gunwale, waved good-bye to my friends of the gendarmerie, and headed the boat for Capernaum to pick up the Sisters. Here I found that they had had a great time. Just as they were in the midst of a mild flirtation with Father Vendelene, who was showing them round his demesne, who should walk in but the Papal Legate, Cardinal Filippo Giustini, just arrived from Rome on a tour of inspection! The good cardinal was not horrified, however, for he insisted on the ladies coming into the Refectory, where he himself poured them out a cup of tea.

On the way back from Capernaum we hugged the west coast of the Lake and made a call at Migdal, an up-to-date Jewish fruit farm on the site of the ancient Magdala, the birthplace of that romantic figure in the New Testament, Mary Magdalene. Unfortunately, the manager, Mr. Glickin, was away, but his representative gave us a delightful tea in the open, under the shade of an enormous fig tree. Here fruits and flowers of all kinds were showered upon us, oranges, pomegranates, bananas, nuts, almonds, etc., all of the most delicious flavour. Our boatmen had much ado in carrying all our gifts down to the shore.

We then skirted the Lake, and when nearing Tiberias saw the caves where the famous Jewish philosopher Maimonides, and the two famous Rabbis, Meir and Ben Akiba, are buried.

Not very far from Tiberias is the pit of Joseph, which old Arabian geographers maintain is the identical one into which the favourite son of Jacob was cast.

Darkness was now swiftly coming on and, as we neared Tiberias, in the twinkling of an eye, a sudden squall burst upon us, and we were glad to reach the little haven in safety.

Altogether it had been a very full day and the Sisters assured me that they would look upon it as one of the red-letter days of their lives.

Before leaving the Sea of Galilee, I made an excursion to the wonderful hot sulphur baths, about three miles to the south of Tiberias, and saw the boiling water gushing out of the cleft in a rock. There is a bathhouse close by where people afflicted with rheumatism dip in these medicinal waters and are made whole again.

On the way back from these springs I passed through the ruins of the old city of Tiberias, with its columns all awry and prostrate, and mounds of débris covering a considerable extent. On a hill, just above the modern Tiberias, stand the ruins of Herod's Palace, and I there saw what is reputed to be the chamber where Herodias' daughter danced for the head of John the Baptist.

In enterprising hands, Tiberias could be made to flourish exceedingly as a winter resort. There one can have excellent boating, fishing, boar-hunting, explorations on horseback through the exceedingly interesting country which surrounds it, and at the same time cure all one's ills in the wonderful hot baths.

Beautiful Palestinian lace is made in this old Hebrew city by industrious Jewish girls, and I brought away some very fine examples of their work.

There is an old synagogue near the Hot Springs where the celebrated Rabbi Meir expounded the law to Israel.

Before I left Galilee I met my old friend, Captain Trumpeldor, who had served under me in the Zion Mule Corps in Gallipoli. I was delighted to see this gallant officer once more, and we had a long chat over old times. Trumpeldor had only just returned from Russia, where he had been organizing a Jewish Legion for service in Palestine. The Bolsheviks, however, interfered with his plans, and he was lucky to escape from their clutches. Sad to relate, a few months after our meeting in Galilee, Captain Trumpeldor met his death there, while defending a Jewish Colony from a raiding party of Bedouins. He directed the defence for two hours after he had been mortally wounded, and then died, fighting to the last. He was one of the most gallant men I have ever met, and his loss is keenly felt by all his friends and comrades.

The Sea of Galilee is bound to have an enormous influence on the economic life of Palestine. Here we have stored up practically an unlimited supply of latent energy. This great mass of water is situated some 700 feet above the level of the Dead Sea, into which its overflow, the Jordan runs.

A canal constructed from the south-west corner of Lake Tiberias, and graded along the Jordan Valley, would, in the length of a few miles, give a vertical fall of over 300 feet. A suitable hydro-electric plant erected at the site of the falls would produce enough energy to revolutionise every phase of life in the Holy Land.

It must be remembered that so far neither coal nor oil have been found in the country, while forests do not exist; consequently the cost of all kinds of fuel is very high, and industrial undertakings, where cheap power is a factor, are out of the question.

What a Heaven-sent boon then is this stored-up energy of the blessed Jordan. Cheap light, heat, and power can be had from it throughout the length and breadth of Palestine. Touch a switch in summer and a whirling fan will keep one's house delightfully cool, while in the winter electrical fires will provide warmth in the chilly evenings on the hill-tops. Evil smelling paraffin lamps and stoves will be a thing of the past, for, of course, electricity will provide all that is necessary in the way of fuel and light.

Ample power is available for the electrification of the existing railways, and, of course, light tramways could be operated all over the country.

Great areas of land now lying fallow could be irrigated and made fruitful and capable of sustaining a large population.

If Palestine is to become a home for any large number of the Jewish people, this great source of economic life must be turned to account, and all the land blessed by the amazing benefits which electricity can shower upon it.

Jewish brains, Jewish capital, and Jewish workers will undoubtedly carry out this scheme, and gradually the country, which is now arid and neglected, will be turned once more into a land flowing with milk and honey. The hills will again be terraced and crowned with fig and olive trees, and the valleys and plains will abound with ripening corn.

The country which for hundreds of years has been at a standstill, lends itself to all kinds of industrial enterprises, such as fruit-farming, olive oil and soap factories, fishing and canning, etc.

The trade and commerce that will flow through Palestine is not to be measured by the paltry revenue returns now shown. When the country is developed, the old trade routes with the hinterland reopened, and the ports at Haifa and Jaffa improved, its importance, commercially, will be enhanced beyond all recognition.

CHAPTER XXXIII

STRANGE METHODS OF THE E.E.F. STAFF

It will be remembered that Lieutenant Jabotinsky was responsible for the idea of forming a Jewish Legion to help England in her great struggle for world freedom.

The British Government was impressed with the possibilities he placed before it, and eventually he was summoned to the War

Office by Lord Derby, then Secretary of State for War, and to the War Cabinet by General Smuts, to expound his proposals. These high officials did not disdain to meet and confer with Jabotinsky on the Jewish Legion question, although at that time he was merely a private soldier, serving in the 20th Battalion of the London Regiment. They knew that he held a very high place in the Zionist movement, and was looked up to by the Jewish masses the world over as one of its most brilliant young leaders.

This fact was also known to the Staff of the E.E.F., but when, as an officer, in August, 1919, Lieutenant Jabotinsky sought an interview with the Commander-in-Chief, hoping that he might induce the local authorities to change their anti-Jewish policy in Palestine, he was not only refused a hearing, but methods were immediately employed to strike him down which I can only describe as despicable and un-English.

Jabotinsky was, of course, pro-British to the core. During his service in Palestine he had been for a time specially attached to the Zionist Commission with the sanction of the Commander-in-Chief. While he was employed in this capacity he brought about the acceptance of a programme by the Jewish Colonists, expressly calling for a British Mandate for Palestine.

All through his military service with the Battalion he, to my personal knowledge, did his utmost to allay the feelings of resentment felt by the Jewish soldiers at the bad treatment they received at the hands of the military authorities, treatment utterly undeserved and uncalled for, but apparently deliberately adopted to further what appeared to be the local policy of making the practical application of the Balfour Declaration an impossibility.

Hostility to all things Jewish was so open, that only those who wilfully shut their eyes could fail to see the game that was being played by certain interested parties. Jabotinsky saw that the line of action adopted must inevitably lead to outbreaks against the Jews, and naturally wanted to ward off such a calamity.

Do not let the reader imagine that there was bad blood between the Palestinian Arabs and the Zionists. That both had dwelt together in unity and concord for over forty years is proof to the contrary.

The anti-Jewish outbreak, which actually took place later on, was carefully fostered, and the hooligan element amongst the Arabs openly encouraged to acts of violence by certain individuals who, for their own ends, hoped to shatter the age-long aspirations of the Jewish people.

There can be no doubt that it was assumed in some quarters that when trouble, which had been deliberately encouraged, arose, the Home Government, embarrassed by a thousand difficulties at its doors, would agree with the wire-pullers in Palestine, and say to the Jewish people that the carrying out of the Balfour Declaration, owing to the hostility displayed by the Arabs, was outside the range of practical politics.

To these schemers it must have been somewhat galling, to say the least of it, to find certain men openly fighting them, foot by foot, and inch by inch, for the realisation of the ideals expressed in the famous Declaration.

One of these men was Jabotinsky, a man with a notable name in Jewry, therefore a thrust at him would also be a blow to Jewish prestige in Palestine. He was a mere foreigner, a Jew from Russia, and presumably without influential friends—a man, surely, on whom officialdom could safely pour out the vials of its unjust wrath, without any fear of evil consequences to itself.

At all events, contemptible methods were adopted in order to strike at the man who had dared to let the authorities know that their local policy was a menace to his people dwelling in the Holy Land, and a serious danger to the Restoration.

When Jabotinsky saw that certain members of the Staff were adopting measures towards Jewish soldiers, and Jewish ideals in Palestine, which must inevitably result in disaster, and being loth to believe that the Commander-in-Chief could be privy to such a policy, he addressed the following letter to General Allenby.

SIR,

I was the initiator of both the Zion Mule Corps and the actual Jewish Battalions. To-day I am forced to witness how my work is breaking into pieces under the intolerable burden of disappointment, despair, broken pledges, and anti-Semitism, permeating the whole administrative and military atmosphere, the hopelessness of all effort and of all devotion.

The common opinion is that you are an enemy of Zionism in general, and of the Jewish Legion in particular. I still try to believe that this is not true, that things happen without your knowledge, that there is a misunderstanding, and that the situation can yet improve.

In this hope, as the last attempt to stop a process which threatens to impair for ever Anglo-Jewish friendship throughout the world, I beg you to grant me a personal interview and permission to speak freely. This letter is entrusted to your chivalry.

(Signed) V. Jabotinsky.

I knew nothing whatever about the despatch of this letter, and although I am aware that red tape will hold up its hands in holy horror at the audacity of it, it must be remembered that Jabotinsky's position was an exceptional one. He was not a British subject, and not used to the routine of British red tape. Members of the British Imperial War Cabinet thought it good policy to hear his views, and, no doubt, when he entrusted this letter to the chivalry of General Allenby, he felt confident that if he was making any deviation from ordinary routine, it was for a good purpose and would not be counted against him.

It is an open, straightforward, honest letter, a heartfelt cry from a man who sees that the whole structure which he has been at such pains to build is in serious peril of being overthrown by the machinations of the anti-Jewish people on the Staff.

And now a curious thing happened. It was known to the Staff that Jabotinsky was at the time staying in Jaffa, and that he was to be found almost daily at the house of a friend who was living there. About a week after he had sent his letter to the Commander-in-Chief, a Staff-Major from G.H.Q., E.E.F., appeared in Jaffa and took up his quarters in the same house as that in which Jabotinsky's friend dwelt. When the inevitable meeting took place, the Staff-Major, who, by the way, knew Jabotinsky well, remarked that the Commander-in-Chief had received his (Jabotinsky's) letter, and would probably send for him one of these days, but that, in the meantime, it would be well if Jabotinsky stated his grievances then and there to himself. "You can speak to me openly as to a friend," said the Major. "I have some influence at G.H.Q., and I shall be glad to assist in righting any wrong done to Jews."

On hearing this, Jabotinsky unhesitatingly explained the situation, both as to its effects on the Regiment and on Jewish aspirations in Palestine. The result of this "friendly conversation" was a mendacious report written by the Staff-Major to the Deputy Adjutant-General at G.H.Q., E.E.F.

Sometime afterwards, by a mere chance, I saw a copy of this report, and so far as it referred to Jabotinsky, it was practically untrue from beginning to end.

If the responsible authorities at G.H.Q. knew of the method adopted to lure Jabotinsky into the "friendly conversation" which served as a pretext for a gross libel on his character, it reminds one of the good old days when Governments had recourse to "Agents provocateurs." What G.H.Q. certainly should have known was that the accusations levelled at Jabotinsky by a member of their Staff were absolutely untrue. They knew him to be a good and gallant officer who had done his duty, and much more than his duty, faithfully and well to England, but it would appear as if they were greedy for such a document and swallowed it with avidity without any reference to me or, so far as I know, to anybody else.

I think that even the most prejudiced of my readers will admit that in fairness and justice to Jabotinsky this secret report should have been submitted to him for his information, and such explanation and refutation as he could give, before any action was taken against him.

It is strictly laid down in the King's Regulations that all adverse reports must be shown to the officer whose reputation is affected, but, as I have shown over and over again, the Staff of the E.E.F. were apparently a law unto themselves and above even King's Regulations!

I knew nothing whatever of all that had been going on; I knew nothing of Jabotinsky's letter to the Commander-in-Chief; I knew nothing of his interview with the Staff-Major from G.H.Q., and, needless to say, I knew nothing of the report which the latter had written.

My first inkling of the situation was through an official letter emanating from the Deputy Adjutant-General, which stated that "the Commander-in-Chief has his own duly constituted advisers on matters of policy and is not prepared to grant an interview to a Lieutenant of the 38th Battalion Royal Fusiliers to discuss such matters."

From this moment G.H.Q. lost no time in getting rid of Jabotinsky. On the 29th August, 1919, I received an urgent order to send this officer to Kantara for immediate demobilization. This took me by surprise, for I was very short of Jewish Officers, and stood much in need of Jabotinsky's services in the Battalion.

I wrote and protested against his demobilization, stating that I needed his services, but the only result was the receipt of the following peremptory memorandum:

"A direct order was conveyed for Lieutenant Jabotinsky to proceed to Demobilization Camp, Kantara, forthwith. If he has not already gone, this officer will leave for Kantara by rail to-day. Non-compliance with this order will lead to disciplinary action being taken. Please report departure."

The above was signed by a Staff Officer.

As a result of this piece of Prussianism, Jabotinsky had to proceed to Kantara, where at lightning speed he was demobilised.

He wrote a protest to the Army Council, which I forwarded with my own views on the case. The appeal was a lengthy one, but I will merely quote the following passage:

140

"With the deepest reluctance and regret I must say that I consider this action shows ingratitude. I do not deserve it at the hands of the British Authorities. From the first days of this War I have worked and struggled for British interests. I am neither a British subject nor an immigrant. I had never been in the United Kingdom or in any British Dominion before this War. I came to England in 1915 as a Russian Journalist, correspondent of the oldest Liberal paper in Russia, the Moscow Wiedomosti. As a correspondent I did my best to explain to the Russian public the British effort and to combat the anti-British propaganda. At the same time I started on my own initiative a pro-Entente and pro-British propaganda amongst neutral and Russian Jewry. At that time many Jews bitterly resented England's alliance with Russia. In the autumn, 1915, I founded a Yiddish fortnightly (Di Tribune) in Copenhagen, which took up a strong anti-German and anti-Turkish attitude. Its articles were constantly quoted in the American Jewish Press, and found their way even into Germany and Austria. Here again I have the right to say that I was one of the few—perhaps one of the two men (counting Dr. Weizmann first)—responsible for the origin of the present pro-British attitude of all Jewry. I may add that I did all this at my own expense, or with means provided by my Zionist friends, without any support from any British source.

Against this I know of no facts which could justify the attitude taken up by G.H.Q., E.E.F. I have never heard of any complaint or censure of my conduct as Officer or Man; I have never been informed or even given a hint that anything in my activity could be objected to.

My compulsory Demobilization under these conditions will throw a slur on my name. I consider it unjust. I request that it be annulled, and that I be reinstated in my well-earned position as an Officer of the Judæans."

A reply to this appeal was never received, and I do not know whether it ever reached the Army Council.

Thus came about the victimization of Jabotinsky, the man who had done so much for England in her hour of need; who had over and over again in the firing line shown that he was prepared to make even the last great sacrifice itself in the cause for which England was fighting. As a reward for all his devotion to England he was, by strange and un-English devices, practically drummed out of the Army.

I think my readers will agree with me that the scandalous course of action pursued by the Staff of the E.E.F. in the case of

Lieutenant Jabotinsky would, if it became popular in high places, soon bring our country to ruin and rob us of our fair name.

We know what the corrupt Bureaucrats have done for the once mighty Russian Empire. Had fair play and justice held sway there we would never have beheld the present orgy of Bolshevism which is sweeping through that unhappy country.

Let all kings, princes, rulers and governors remember that to "do justice and ensue it" makes the stoutest barrier against Bolshevism, for, as it says in Ecclesiastes, "oppression maketh a wise man mad."

CHAPTER XXXIV

THE FIRST JUDÆANS

Nothing but a sense of the duty which I owed to my officers and men induced me to continue serving in such a hostile atmosphere after the armistice had been declared.

We suffered, but we suffered in silence, and just "carried on."

In the midst of our tribulations we, however, scored a decided triumph, for the year-old decision of the War Office was at last announced by the local Staff that we had won a special name, viz., the Judæans, and that H.M. the King had sanctioned the Menorah as a special badge for the Battalion.

The withholding of this information from us for a full year could not have been an oversight, for I had repeatedly written to ask if the War Office had not sanctioned this name and badge for the Battalion, but received no reply. I can only presume that the object of G.H.Q. in withholding this information, which would have brought prestige to the Jews, was that they had hoped to get the Battalion disbanded and abolished so that it might never have the gratification of knowing that the Imperial Authorities considered that the Jewish Battalion had distinguished itself, and was therefore entitled to the special name and badge promised in 1917 by Lord Derby when Secretary of State for War.

Just after we had received this good news, I was gladdened by receiving from the Council of Jews at Jerusalem a beautifully illuminated parchment scroll, thanking me for the stand I had made in upholding the ideals expressed in the Balfour Declaration, and for having led the Jewish Battalions successfully in the great struggle which resulted in the "Crown of Victory."

Yet one more triumph was in store for the 1st Judæans, for, in the beginning of December, 1919, orders came from the War Office that it was to be retained to garrison Palestine, and that the 39th and 40th Battalions were to be amalgamated with it.

It was a great satisfaction to me to learn that it was to be retained, for a time at least, as a unit of the British Army, and that it was to be officially known as the First Judæans Battalion.

I now felt that my work was done and I could chant my "Nunc Dimittis." I had seen my child weather the storms which had beaten so fiercely about it, and in the end specially chosen to garrison its own Home Land.

A permanent force of Judæans in Palestine is an essentially sound measure from every point of view.

World Jewry would, I am sure, be willing to take the entire cost of the maintenance of this Force on its own shoulders; the money spent on it would be well invested, for it would be the training centre of Palestinian volunteers. Such a training would instil a sense of responsibility, and enable young Jewry the more readily to follow steadfastly in the simple but sublime footsteps of their heroic forefathers.

As soon as I got back to England, I had an interview with the Adjutant-General at the War Office, and requested that the savage sentences passed on the young Americans at Belah should be revised. Although the Adjutant-General was most sympathetic, he could not, at the moment, see his way to interfere, so I then wrote to the Prime Minister to let him know that these American soldiers had been very harshly treated and were still imprisoned in the Citadel at Cairo. I pointed out that it was hardly sound policy to offend a powerful ally by inflicting such a barbarous sentence on men who had come over the seas as volunteers to help us in the Great War. I therefore begged him to have their case investigated.

The result of this letter was that the men were speedily released and went back to their homes in the United States.

CHAPTER XXXV

THE JERUSALEM POGROM

Shortly after my return to England events occurred in Palestine which prove up to the hilt all that I have written with regard to the anti-Jewish attitude of certain members of the E.E.F. Staff.

A veritable "pogrom," such as we have hitherto only associated with Tsarist Russia, took place in the Holy City of Jerusalem in April, 1920, and as this was the climax to the maladministration of the Military Authorities, I consider that the facts of the case should be made public.

To the observant onlooker it was quite evident that the hostile policy pursued by the Administration must inevitably lead to outbreaks against the Jews. An intelligent people, such as the Arabs, could not be blind to the anti-Jewish course being steered.

The Balfour Declaration, that divinely inspired message to the people of Israel, was never allowed to be officially published within the borders of Palestine; the Hebrew language was proscribed; there was open discrimination against the Jews; the Jewish Regiment was at all times kept in the background and treated as a pariah. This official attitude was interpreted by the hooligan element and interested schemers in the only possible way, viz., that the military authorities in Palestine were against the Jews and Zionism, and the conviction began to grow, in some native minds at least, that any act calculated to deal a death blow to Zionist aspirations would not be unwelcome to those in authority in the Holy Land.

Moreover, this malign influence was sometimes strengthened by very plain speaking. The Military Governor of an important town was actually heard to declare in a Y.M.C.A. Hut, in the presence of British and French Officers, and of Arab waiters, that in case of anti-Jewish riots in his city, he would remove the garrison and take up his position at a window, where he could watch, and laugh at, what went on!

This amazing declaration was reported to the Acting Chief Administrator, and the Acting Chief Political Officer, but no action was taken against the Governor. Only one interpretation can be placed on such leniency.

In March, 1920, the following extraordinary order was issued to the troops in Palestine:—"As the Government has to pursue in Palestine a policy unpopular with the majority of the population, trouble may be expected to arise between the Jews and the Arabs." This wording is very significant. It was obviously calculated to throw the blame for any trouble on the Jews, at the same time representing the Government as an unfortunate victim, who, under some mysterious pressure, "has to pursue" a Zionist policy.

The moment I heard that a certain officer was to be appointed to an important post in Palestine I felt it my duty to warn the Chief Zionist leader of the evil that would follow such an appointment, and told him that in the interests not only of Jewry, but of England, it was necessary that he should make a public protest against the appointment of this official. Although I warned Dr. Weizmann of the dangers that would follow, he was loth to believe that a British Officer would be disloyal to the policy laid down by his Government. The good Doctor had not suffered with the Jewish Battalion and did not realize the situation or the intrigues that were in the air. So far as I am aware, no protest was made and this official was duly appointed. I feared for the future, not so much on account of the Jews, as on account of the harm that would be done to the prestige and good name of England, and the result will show that my fears were only too well grounded.

Within a few months of this appointment, public anti-Zionist demonstrations were permitted throughout the land. These manifestations took the form of processions through the streets with drums beating and banners flying, the chanting of fanatical verses against the Jews being a feature of these displays. In Jaffa inflammatory speeches were delivered from the steps of the Military Governor's office, in the presence of British officials, calling for the extermination of Zionism.

Arab papers were allowed to write the most outrageous articles against the Jews, while on the other hand, if a Jewish paper dared to say the least word of protest, it was immediately called to account.

With these significant happenings taking place before their eyes, and feeling that they would get little or no protection from the Military Administration, the Jews clearly saw that it was absolutely essential for their own safety to form a Self-Defence Corps, for purely protective purposes. This they did, and Lieutenant Jabotinsky was entrusted with the command. This officer, with the full knowledge of the Administration, enrolled a body of young men and trained them in case of need.

His first act on taking command was to inform the Authorities

145

of the Corps' existence, its arming, and its purpose. He even asked the Government for weapons, reminding them that rifles and ammunition had been issued to Jewish Colonists in Galilee under similar circumstances. It must be remembered that the Jewish people in Palestine never gave the Authorities a moment's anxiety; on the contrary, they were most law-abiding citizens, who helped the British Administration in every conceivable way. They were astounded and mystified by the hostility displayed towards them by the local Military Administration, and it is not too much to say that they went in fear of their lives, for the hooligan element in the Arab quarter began to declare openly that they would slaughter them.

The day when an outbreak on the part of the cut-throats was expected was Friday, 2nd April, for on that date the celebrated "Nebi Musa" procession was to take place. Moslems from all parts of Palestine meet once a year for prayer at the Mosque of Omar (built on the site of Solomon's temple), and then form a procession to the Tomb of Moses in the Jordan Valley, near the Dead Sea. The Moslem world holds Moses in great veneration as a Prophet, and believes that when he died on Mount Nebo, a Bedouin carried his body across the Jordan and buried it at the shrine now known as Nebi Musa, which is annually visited by thousands of Moslem pilgrims.

The day dreaded by the Jews passed without incident, but in the light of what took place a couple of days later, I am inclined to think that this desirable result was achieved, not so much by the precautions taken by the Administration, as by those taken by the Jewish Self-Defence Corps, which was known to be held in readiness for all eventualities on that day.

On Sunday, 4th April, a belated crowd of pilgrims from Hebron approached the Holy City by the Jaffa Gate. Fanatical agitators posted themselves on the balcony of the Municipality Building and, for the space of two hours, delivered brutally inflammatory speeches against the Jews to this mob, in the presence of British officials who understood Arabic. It must be remembered that these pilgrims were armed, and yet no attempt was made to suppress the agitators, although there was ample police and military strength available in the neighbourhood.

Immediately after the inflammatory speeches, acts of violence began.

I reproduce here extracts from a couple of letters which I received, giving graphic descriptions of the outbreak by eyewitnesses, one of them a Senior British Officer, not a Jew:

146

PALESTINE,
10th April, 1920.

MY DEAR COLONEL,

We are passing through terrible and unprecedented times. Who could ever have thought that a pogrom "à la Russe," with all its horrors, could take place in Jerusalem under British rule! Who could ever have conceived that it should be possible, in the Holy City of Jerusalem, that for three days Jews, old and young, women and children could be slaughtered; that rape should be perpetrated, Synagogues burnt, scrolls of the Law defiled, and property plundered right and left, under the banner of England!

The anti-Jewish feeling of the Administration here you, of course, know all about, as you have experienced it yourself, but latterly the notorious Syria Genuba (an Arab daily in Jerusalem) printed day after day inflammatory articles against the Jews....

Anti-Jewish demonstrations were allowed to take place and inflammatory speeches were allowed to be made against the Jews. The evil men amongst the Arabs openly declared that they would slaughter the Jews at the Festival of Nebi Musa. The Government was warned by the Jewish press, and by Jewish responsible leaders, but these were not listened to, and, as a matter of fact, the Feast was proclaimed with great pomp, Lord Allenby and Major-General Louis Jean Bols, the Chief Administrator, being present....

(Signed) XX.

PALESTINE,
11th April, 1920.

MY DEAR COLONEL,

... with my wife I went up to Jerusalem to spend the Easter week-end, and a very nice week-end it surely was! Long before this letter reaches you, you will have learned something of the happenings in the Holy City, but as my wife and I saw the first blow struck, and had very personal experience of the immediately ensuing bother, you may be interested.

The happenings here have raised all sorts of questions, and while for the moment the trouble is over, I fear the end is not yet.

On the morning of Easter Sunday we were standing on the balcony of the New Grand Hotel watching the progress of an Arab procession just arrived from Hebron. As the procession reached the entrance to the Jaffa Gate it just had the appearance of the usual show of this kind—a bit noisy, but apparently well-behaved. It was escorted by two officers of the Military Administration and a few

147

of the Arab police. All at once the members of the procession formed themselves into a square, just inside the gate, and the first thing we saw then was an old Jew, about 70 years of age, get his head split open with an Arab's sword, and as soon as he was down he was stoned; within a few minutes a lot more Jews got like treatment. By this time the crowd was well out of hand and rushed quickly into the old City looting and killing, and a few hours afterwards there was a steady evacuation of battered Jews. There was no military present.

The following day the trouble started again, and a lot more were injured, and the third morning there was more looting and more casualties, and then at last the military took strong steps and the trouble was at an end.

Yours sincerely,
(Signed) E.N.

In less than half an hour from the beginning of the outbreak, two companies of the Self-Defence Corps marched to the Jaffa and Damascus Gates to assist in quelling the disturbance within the walls, but they found the gates closed to them and held by British troops. It is very significant that within a few minutes of the commencement of the pogrom, British troops held all the gates of the city, with explicit orders to allow no one in and no one out—not even helpless women, fleeing from the horrors that were being enacted in the Jewish quarter, unless they held special permits.

For nearly three days the work of murder, rape, sacrilege, and pillage went on practically unchecked—all under British rule. There is only one word which fittingly describes the situation, and that is the Russian word "pogrom." It means a semi-lawful attack on Jews. The assailants believe that they may murder, rape, burn and loot to their hearts' content, with the silent blessing of the authorities, and it is a very significant fact that all through this Jerusalem pogrom the hooligans' cry was "El dowleh ma ana," which means "The Government is with us." The attackers were absolutely convinced of the truth of their battle cry.

During these three terrible days several Jews were killed, hundreds were wounded (many of these being old men, women and children), rape was perpetrated, Synagogues were burnt, and tens of thousands of pounds worth of Jewish property was looted or destroyed.

The pogrom was confined to that part of Jerusalem within the walls of the old City, where the Moslems greatly outnumber the Jews—in fact the latter are here a small and helpless minority. They take no part in politics, not even in political Zionism, but are

148

absorbed in religious practices and observances, and abhor all things worldly. Even self-defence is repellent to them, and all forms of violence anathema.

These harmless people dwell in half-a-dozen narrow tortuous streets and bazaars, in one corner of the old City. This Jewish quarter is quite easy to defend. A few armed men posted at the narrow entrances could hold any mob at bay. Why did not the military authorities see that this was done? It was not until the third day that effective action was taken. In the meantime, hell was let loose on these unfortunate people. Even the wretched few who got to the City gates, unless they possessed special permits, were refused permission to escape and were forced to return to the devilries being enacted by the murdering, raping, looting mob.

It is a black page in our history, and those responsible should not be allowed to escape just punishment.

To cover their own blunders the local Administration looked round for a scapegoat, and arrested Jabotinsky and some score members of the Jewish Self-Defence Corps.

Jabotinsky was tried on a ridiculous charge of "banditism, instigating the people of the Ottoman Empire to mutual hatred, pillage, rapine, devastation of the country, and homicide in divers places"—in fact the Ottoman penal code was ransacked to trump up these absurd charges against him. Jabotinsky had been guilty of nothing except that he had organised the Self-Defence Corps with the full knowledge of the authorities, many weeks before the outbreak, and it was owing to the existence of this Corps that the pogrom did not take much more serious dimensions. By far the greater part of the Jews, and practically all the Zionist Jews, dwell outside the old City in the modern part of Jerusalem, and it would naturally be upon these that the mob would have fallen, but not a Jewish house outside the City walls was raided, for the simple reason that the Jewish Self-Defence Corps was there and ready to act.

The Self-Defence Corps did nothing whatever against the British Authorities, and many members of it were in fact used by the Administration to police the environs of the City. Nevertheless, a British Military Court, which publicly stated that it would be bound by no rules of procedure, was found, which convicted Jabotinsky, and inflicted upon him the savagely vindictive sentence of FIFTEEN YEARS' PENAL SERVITUDE!

This trumping up of the preposterous charges mentioned is a disgrace to British Justice, and the whole history of this atrocious outrage is a foul stain on our fair fame.

It may be noted in passing that two Arabs caught raping

Jewish girls during the pogrom received the same sentence as Jabotinsky, whose only crime was that he was a Jew.

Jabotinsky was cast into prison, clothed in prison garb, had his hair cropped, and was marched in company with the two Arabs convicted of rape through Jerusalem and Kantara, places where he was well known as a British officer. Even the worst Hun that we have read of could hardly have exceeded the savagery and tyranny shown by the Military Authorities of the E.E.F. towards Jabotinsky, an officer who fought stoutly for us and helped England and her cause in every possible way to the full extent of his power during the War.

Of course a storm of public indignation was aroused. In fact one of our leading Statesmen, on seeing the telegram announcing the barbarous sentence, was heard to remark:—

"The Military in Palestine must have gone mad."

The matter was raised in the House of Commons, and Mr. Churchill, who was then Secretary of State for War, was called upon to make a statement. The War Office took action and, in a very short time, the sentence was annulled.

It apparently required this outrage to open the eyes of the Home Government to what was going on in Palestine. As soon as they realised the situation, matters began to move in the right direction, and one of the first steps taken was the removal of the Military Administration which had failed so hopelessly to carry out the policy of the Imperial Government.

CHAPTER XXXVI

THE DAWN

While Jerusalem was yet plunged in sorrow and filled with lamentation, the glad tidings arrived from San Remo that the Allied Council had endorsed England's promise of a National Home for the Jews in Palestine, and that Great Britain had been appointed the Mandatory Power.

England, to emphasize her determination to deal justly with

Israel, wisely decided that the ruler of Palestine should be a Jew, and appointed Sir Herbert Samuel as first High Commissioner of the Holy Land.

When the great roll-call is made of those who have helped in bringing about the Restoration, the name of Baron Edmund de Rothschild will take a high and honourable place. His boundless munificence to the Zionist cause and to the Zionist Colonists in Palestine has helped the movement enormously.

Palestine will loom larger and larger in world importance as the years roll by. We have seen that it is the very keystone of our policy in the Near and Far East, and when it is colonized by a friendly people working hand in hand with England then the vexed question of our interests in those regions will be solved.

There is plenty of room in Palestine for both Jew and Arab, and, in fact, one is the complement of the other. At present there are about 650,000 Arabs in the country, but when Palestine is watered and tilled and made a fruitful country once again, it will support a population of five or six millions of people.

Not only would the Jews not injure the Arabs, but, on the contrary, Jewish colonization and Jewish enterprise will prove extremely beneficial to all the dwellers in Palestine.

The Jewish immigrants now going into the country are full of boundless enthusiasm, ready to work and give even life itself to bring about the reconstruction of their ancient Homeland.

With Jewish brains, Jewish labour, and Jewish capital, Palestine will be made to flourish like the proverbial green bay tree. The land will be irrigated and afforested; water power will be "harnessed" and made to supply light and heat. Trade of all sorts will spring up, fresh markets for goods will be opened, the wonderful natural harbour of Haifa will be improved—and all of this will naturally bring increased wealth and comfort to the Arab as well as to the Jew.

Even at the present moment the Jewish colonies are a joy to behold, and the land in their immediate neighbourhood has gone up in value threefold.

For many years the Jew and the Arab have worked together without the slightest friction, and I see no reason for any in the future. There will be no trouble whatever in Palestine between these two peoples when the country is properly governed, and the local officials loyally carry out the policy of the Imperial Government.

With an efficient straightforward Administration, holding the scales of Justice evenly, and working in co-operation with Jew and Arab, the dawn of a new and prosperous era for the Holy Land is assured, and Israel's age-long aspirations will at last be fulfilled.

Britain's share towards the fulfilment of prophecy must, however, not be forgotten, and the names of Mr. Lloyd George and Sir Arthur Balfour, two men who were raised up to deal justly with Israel, will, I feel sure, live for all time in the hearts and affections of the Jewish people. It is owing to the stimulus given by the Balfour Declaration to the soul of Jewry throughout the world that we are now looking upon the wonderful spectacle unfolding itself before our eyes, of the people of Israel returning to the Land promised to Abraham and his seed for ever.

In the ages to come it will always redound to the glory of England that it was through her instrumentality that the Jewish people were enabled to return and establish their National Home in the Promised Land.

"Weeping may endure for a night, but joy cometh in the morning."

www.ingramcontent.com/pod-product-compliance
Lightning Source LLC
Chambersburg PA
CBHW010237100426
42813CB00041B/3482/J